EVELYN JACKS'
FAMILY TAX ESSENTIALS

KNOW MORE. KEEP MORE.

How to Build a Wealth Purpose with a Tax Strategy

KNOWLEDGE BUREAU
NEWSBOOKS

A VIBRANT INTERACTIVE EDUCATIONAL EXPERIENCE

Evelyn Jacks

Evelyn Jacks' **FAMILY TAX ESSENTIALS: Know More. Keep More.**
How to Build a Wealth Purpose with a Tax Strategy

Knowledge Bureau Report: A free subscription to this national electronic publication will help readers stay up-to-date with news at Canada Revenue Agency, Finance Canada and the consequences of financial and economic developments in Canada and around the world. To subscribe and participate in opinion polls, go to www.knowledgebureau.com.

Follow Evelyn Jacks on Twitter @evelynjacks

Printed and bound in Canada

Library and Archives Canada Cataloguing in Publication

Jacks, Evelyn, author
Family tax essentials : know more, keep more : how to
build a wealth purpose with a tax strategy/ Evelyn Jacks.

Includes index.
ISBN 978-1-927495-30-8 (paperback)

1. Income shifting (Taxation)--Canada--Popular works.
2. Family--Taxation--Canada--Popular works. 3. Tax planning--Canada--Popular works. I. Title.

HJ4661.J2125 2015   343.7105'23   C2015-907954-3

Published by:
Knowledge Bureau, Inc.
187 St. Mary's Road, Winnipeg, Manitoba, Canada, R2H 1J2
204-953-4769 www.knowledgebureau.com
reception@knowledgebureau.com

Research and Editorial Assistance: Walter Harder and Associates,
Cover and Page Design: Evelyn Jacks, Karen Armstrong Graphic Design

ACKNOWLEDGEMENTS

I would like to thank my son, Cordell, for the inspiration to write this book.

I am blessed by the talented contributions of my research assistant and editor, Walter Harder, and the outstanding artistic achievements of Karen Armstrong. A big thank you is also in order to my "work family" – every wonderful soul at Knowledge Bureau – and in particular, Michelle Clarke. Their dedication makes a work of this kind possible.

Sincerely

Evelyn

PRESIDENT, KNOWLEDGE BUREAU
EVELYN JACKS

Evelyn is Canada's most respected educator in tax and financial literacy and one of Canada's most prolific financial authors. She has penned 52 books, including bestsellers *Jacks on Tax, Essential Tax Facts* and *Make Sure It's Deductible*. She was recently named one of the Top 25 Women of Influence in Canada for the second time.

Evelyn is also the Founder and President of Knowledge Bureau, Canada's leading national educational institute for continuing professional development in the tax and financial services. Evelyn has developed curricula for hundreds of certificate courses, and the prestigious MFA™ (Master Financial Advisor) and DFA-Tax and Bookkeeping Services Specialist Designations.

Evelyn has been influential in advising governments on tax and financial literacy policies. She was appointed by former Finance Minister Flaherty to the Federal Task Force on Financial Literacy, and by the former Premier of Manitoba, Gary Filmon, to the Lower Tax Commission, to advise on the direction of the provincial tax regime. Recently she has co-founded the Manitoba Financial Literacy Forum in partnership with the Manitoba Securities Commission, dedicated to increase financial literacy in that province.

She is also a well-known national commentator, keynote speaker and budget analyst who has written thousands of articles, and spent countless hours teaching average Canadians about their rights and opportunities in filing tax returns, volunteering her time on newscasts, chatrooms and talk shows from coast-to-coast, reaching millions of listeners.

Evelyn has been a role model for women in business. Amongst her accomplishments, Evelyn is a past President of the Manitoba Club, Western Canada's oldest private business club and the recipient of the Rotman School of Business Canadian Woman Entrepreneur of the Year Award.

TABLE OF CONTENTS

FAMILY TAX ESSENTIALS

PART 4 SAVE – WITH TAX-ASSISTANCE

PART 5 GROW – MANAGE YOUR MONEY BUCKETS

PART 6 PRESERVE – LIVE YOUR WEALTH PURPOSE

PART 7 ESSENTIAL FAMILY TAX FACTS _____ 210

PART 1 – STRATEGIZE

THE ODDS ARE
IN YOUR
FAVOUR

Most average people have neither a Wealth Purpose nor a Tax Strategy for achieving it. Those who do, will be well positioned to build significant wealth in a century that promises dramatic change.

What is a Wealth Purpose? It's a finite goal, to help you achieve financial freedom. When you add a Tax Strategy, you'll reach your finish line faster, and that's very important in today's economic environment.

Consider this: total global wealth grew to a new record level between mid-2013 and mid-2014, increasing to more than twice the U.S. dollar level recorded in the year 2000.[1] In fact, from 2000 to 2014, global wealth increased 125%, despite the most devastating financial crisis since the Great Depression of the last century.

For people with wealth, that's a trend that is expected to continue, at least in the short term. By 2019, global median wealth will rise by 36%, and the number of millionaires in the world will increase by 50% – the fastest growing category of all wealth holders.[2]

Is it possible for you to join this group? The answer is: absolutely! Research tells us that most millionaires are self-made,[3] and that's true also of the world's billionaires – 60% of them have made their wealth themselves.

You too can decide to be "self-made" when it
comes to your financial future.

---

[1] According to the Research Department at Credit Suisse, which releases its *Global Wealth Report* annually every October.

[2] Ibid

[3] WealthX Report, June 13, 2014.

That's the good news. Here's the reality check: to join the millionaires club – and we will show you how to do that in this book – it will pay to have a deliberate plan, to aim higher in setting your personal and financial goals and to try to achieve them faster than the norm, by paying attention to your tax advantages.

Multiplying your personal productivity with every possible invest-ment advantage is also becoming increasingly important. Canadians, like millions in the Western World, are in the midst of new challenges that change everything: a massive demographic shift. Economic ac-tivity – and tax revenues – shrink as the majority of taxpayers retire. This could impact younger taxpayers in the near future, as their num-bers are smaller than the baby boomers.

For the first time, Canada's 65 year olds have outnumbered children ages 0 to 14: just over 18% of the baby boomers had turned 65 by July 1, 2015. Statistics Canada forecasts that the 65 year olds will grow to 20.1% of the population by 2024, while the number of young children will remain relatively stable at 16.3%. In both the U.S. and Canada, the Millennials (the under 35 year olds) are starting to outnumber the boomers in the workforce for the first time.

In this environment of depopulation when fewer, younger taxpayers face the burden of paying most of the taxes, while looking after both the elderly and minors, it's much more difficult to accumulate assets for their future, and get good returns on their investments.

These demographic changes are affecting many countries around the world at the same time, and can negatively affect consumer demand, corporate profits and asset values. This was predicted in an interesting report back in January 2002, *Depopulation and Ageing in Europe and Japan: The Hazardous Transition to a Labour Shortage Economy.*[4] It's worth the read, if you're so inclined.

Short strokes: a family's wealth can drop significantly when financial or housing markets fluctuate as a result of population declines. The financial negatives are worse when there is too much debt. Govern-ments are affected too: slowing economic activity results in fewer tax dollars to pay for important social benefits. In Canada, a smaller base of working taxpayers will be forced to pay more for rising senior-related costs like the Old Age Security (OAS), for example. This line item alone will balloon from $46 billion today to $109 billion by 2040.

---

[4] By Paul S. Hewitt

*Future wealth holders recognize
that there are opportunities in times of great change.
Hesitating, however, can produce a more difficult road.*

If you live in Canada, you already have a healthy head start to building great wealth. We are fortunate that only 3.5% of Canadian family units have little or no wealth. It is also clear who these people are and that their circumstances are not necessarily permanent. According to Statistics Canada:[5]

- **The Young: 15- to 34-year-olds.** Money management and savings skills are critical to this cohort, who set spending and saving habits in these formative years. The young have a singular advantage over everyone else: time. When you have both time and money, your odds of becoming wealthier multiply significantly, especially with the right financial principles in place.

- **The Uneducated.** These are people who haven't achieved a high-school diploma. Education is critical to financial success later in life; a key factor in the ability to earn sufficient income to buy a home and invest in the financial markets.

- **Singles.** Unattached individuals and lone-parent families have the most difficulty accumulating wealth. It's important to think carefully about the financial circumstances in which a family is raised and for society to help with opportunities for education, housing, child care and meaningful work.

*Simply put, educated people make more money
and accumulate more wealth.*

They are able to get better jobs and buy a home. This has tax advantages, too: every household in Canada can own one tax exempt personal residence. That means, if you buy a home you reside in at some time of the year, and sell it for $100,000 more than you paid for it, you can pocket 100% of that gain.

*You will be wealthier, in other words,
when you own a tax exempt principal residence.*

---

[5] Statistics Canada, March 23, 2015, Canadian Financial Capability Survey

But, mortgage debt represents the majority of all debt in Canada. It's difficult to establish a long term Wealth Purpose when all your eggs are in one, very expensive basket. So many people live paycheque to paycheque when they have "too much house" and miss opportunities to diversify their financial holdings, and therefore their income sources.

It's a bad move to buy too much house; unless you can leverage your investment to earn or own more.

Buying two houses for the price of one, for example, or a multi-dwelling home is an option that could create rental income. Should real estate values fluctuate downward as a result of depopulation, more of those opportunities may arise, providing for an investment income source that multiples your singular energy. It's a smart move (if you can afford to hang on until real estate values appreciate again) to generate gains on one tax exempt property and revenues from one taxable investment property.

When you have a Wealth Purpose and a Tax Strategy for getting there, you'll find opportunities in the financial markets too, and be more deliberate about how you use your money, in general. You will be fine, despite the financial obstacles that will come your way, if you save well. In fact, you'll exceed the norm.

The Money Moral

It's going to be tougher to manage emerging financial risks without deliberate financial goals, accompanied by tax efficiency. Fortunately, those with a Wealth Purpose and a Tax Strategy will do extremely well, as global wealth trends indicate.

WHERE
BREAKTHROUGHS HAPPEN

Most people worry about one singular concept in their financial future, and frankly, it's crippling in its effect on their quality of life: "Will I have enough...?" It seems to take a lot of money to "feel" like you do.

You may be surprised to know that the majority (72%) of people worth $1 to $5 million don't feel wealthy. That means there are millionaires walking the streets today[1] who don't have financial peace of mind. It appears to take $5 million before people feel wealthy. Quite a phenomenon, isn't it?

What's your number?

When will you feel that you have financial peace of mind?

What will it take for you to understand, intrinsically, that you don't have to worry about money anymore? How will you know when you have arrived at the number that makes you comfortable? When you have decided on it, that's your Wealth Purpose. That's the definitive number that means "Enough" to you.

Only when their *Wealth Purpose has been achieved*, can most people truly focus on using their financial resources to enjoy their life to the fullest. They will give themselves permission to retire sooner or to pursue their *Life Purpose*. What's amazing is that for some people, understanding that they can achieve their Wealth Purpose allows them to self-actualize along the way.

This is not just about having money, in other words.

---

[1] *UBS Investor Watch*, 4,450 U.S. investors responded to a survey from June 23–July 1, 2013.

In defining and taking control of the journey to your Wealth Purpose, consider this quote from the author of *Rich Dad, Poor Dad*, Robert Kiyosaki:

> *"I am concerned that too many people are focused too much on money and not on their greatest wealth, which is their education.... If they think money will solve the problems, I am afraid those people will have a rough ride. Intelligence solves problems and produces money. Money without financial intelligence is money soon gone."*

Breakthroughs happen, when people focus on the right stuff, and that takes a strategy and a process. That's as true of building wealth as it is of reaching athletic or academic goals. Having a wealth plan that is comprehensive is important. You will want to think about the concerns even multi-millionaires have about their future – things like long term health care or supporting their grandchildren – because those details will help you feel confident about your future, too.

People who have a Wealth Purpose, go a step farther. They develop principles to guide them in all things financial: how they make their money, and how they manage the money they make. They empower their personal work efforts by assigning specific purposes to their income, their savings and their spending. They give each dollar a specific job, and a specific "home", empowering their money to work harder than they do, to secure their financial future.

Along the way, they establish an acceptable cost of living, but not at the expense of their two precious resources: time and money.

How to best begin? Benchmarking your Personal Net Worth (PNW) is key. Then use this number as your definitive success marker in reaching your Wealth Purpose. Over your lifetime, measuring your PNW periodically becomes an accountable scorecard.

Your PNW is the difference between the value of your assets and your liabilities.

This can be sobering exercise for some, but usually it's an exhilarating one, as most people don't know how wealthy they really are. You may be closer to your Wealth Purpose than you think. Living in the blissful state of self-actualization; that is, with financial freedom, may be just around the corner.

What's your net worth today?

Try defining it at the end of this section of the book. Remember, net worth increases when you acquire new assets or reduce your debt; to that end, it checks up on your financial behaviors. What would you like your PNW to be 5 years from now? 30 years from now?

What will it be when you have reached your Wealth Purpose?

Wealth grows when you choose to spend less than you make and invest in assets that will appreciate in value relative to your cost of investment. That's also when acceptable rates of return on your earnings become obvious. These numbers will always tell you a true story of your progress; but they become truer, when you understand *tax efficiency*.

Tax efficiency is the process of taking advantage of tax rules to pay the least amount of taxes on income, in order to accumulate, grow and preserve the most after-tax wealth for the family over time.

What's important is what you keep... after taxes, inflation and the cost of investing.

Tax efficiency will make every dollar work harder and faster – because tax savings can return up to 50% and more, depending on your tax bracket. Impressive gains, yet most people leave them on the table.

That's why a Tax Strategy is as important as your Wealth Purpose. Giving every dollar a job in the right "tax home", helps you to prioritize how, when and where you save, supercharging your financial journey into the stratosphere. In fact, you may arrive at your Wealth Purpose twice as quickly as those who ignore their tax choices.

The Money Moral

Own your Wealth Purpose, and the glue that holds your choices together: your Tax Strategy. Those who add tax efficiency to the mix can achieve their Wealth Purpose more quickly.

NOTES: *My Wealth Purpose*

BUILD YOUR TAX STRATEGY
WITH EXPERT HELP

There are six essential steps in building a Tax Strategy to complement your Wealth Purpose:

1. **STRATEGIZE:** Create Your Wealth Plan

2. **COMPLY:** Get Expert Tax Help

3. **CONSUME:** With Low-Taxed Dollars

4. **SAVE:** With Tax Assistance

5. **GROW:** Manage Your Money Buckets

6. **PRESERVE:** Live Your Wealth Purpose

To make sure everyone is on the same page with your Wealth Purpose, you will need a different solution to tax and financial advice from the norm. While you do need to execute on specific transactions, filing a tax return for example or making specific investments, the truth is that technology has made it all so easy, you could do it yourself. So why would you pay for help?

One reason is help in joint decision-making about life events, as well as financial events. The old adage says that "money can't buy happiness." This is statistically true. In an article published June 2, 2015, by the OECD,[1] "The Recipe for a Better Life," reveals that people around the world are increasingly finding their happiness in things other than money, but having money helps. Income and wealth are key factors in enhancing overall quality of life.

---

[1] The Organization for Economic Cooperation and Development (OECD) started in 1960 and consists of 34 economically linked democracies plus over 70 more non-member economies dedicated to promote economic growth and sustainable development.

People who build wealth soon bump into our complex financial world and the various services and fees that operation within it. Advisors often operate in silos; accountants, lawyers, investment advisors each executing different financial transactions. Clients are often left in the position of explaining what one has done to the other, hearing conflicting advice along the way.

This speaks well to the need for one key advisor who will help you co-ordinate the six essential steps to your Wealth Purpose, with all the specialists needed along the way to execute on the plan. Look for a knowledgeable and empathetic leader who can perform a three-part role:

Educator. Tax advisors and financial advisors working together have an important role to play in counselling their clients in the principles of Real Wealth Management™[2] – how to accumulate, grow, preserve and transition wealth with sustainability. This is a great investment in the future growth and transition of the family wealth they may be accounting for today. Top three things you are looking for in a financial educator:

1. **Builds Your Confidence**. There is no such thing as a stupid tax or financial question. If you are going to be the leader in charge of your Wealth Purpose, your key job is to probe and understand. Your educational mentors must be prepared to explain terminology, concepts and strategies to you in a way that puts you at ease and allows you to understand how you will best execute on the choices you have to make. This person will help you set your goals, keep you focused on them, and provide real advice: experience, wisdom, judgements and opinions for you to consider.

2. **Builds Your Skills.** You're going to have to know some hard facts about taxes and investing that are a prerequisite to decision-making. Your key advisors will define, explain and provide examples of pros and cons. They will also ask you several open-ended questions to make you think about the decisions you need to make. Most of all they will challenge you to consider your decisions in relation to the collaborative strategy you have set for achieving your Wealth Purpose.

---

[2] A framework for developing strategy and process in the execution of a family wealth management plan, pioneered by Knowledge Bureau, a national Canadian educational institute focused on excellence in financial education.

Advocate. Income counts when accumulating assets and in managing debt. Look for relationships with tax and financial advisors who are interested in working hard with the whole family to create more after-tax income that can be put to work to acquire assets and manage debt. However, the top three attributes of advocates who work for your family are people who can do the following:

1. **Keep You on Track**. These folks are sounding boards when there are events that trigger you to make decisions about your money – life events like births and deaths; financial events like a new career opportunity or early retirement; and economic events like currency and market fluctuations that make you swoon.

2. **Manage Risks to Your Wealth**. Managing risk to your tax and financial affairs is the primary job of your financial advocate, no matter his or her area of specialization. You want the best person for the job when a tax auditor comes to the door. But mostly, you want to avoid the tax audit. That's why it's important to work with a tax advisor who is careful to file an audit-proof return with you at the start. When it comes to your financial planners and advisors, work with people who have a long term view with you.

3. **Connect You with Expertise**. None of us can know everything. That's why a well-connected advisor who can bring specialized solutions when you need them is very valuable. It's important to reserve for yourself the opportunity to work with the very best people when you need them – when you are at your most vulnerable in making difficult decisions.

Steward. "The careful and responsible management of something entrusted to one's care..." That's the definition of stewardship from the Merriam-Webster Dictionary. Growing healthy, well-educated children is the job of parents. Growing healthy, tax-efficient financial portfolios that withstand the test of time to result in sustainable wealth is the work of a dedicated family wealth advisor. That's different from a "financial advisor" who is providing product solutions in the absence of a family wealth plan. Top three attributes include:

1. **Selflessness**. Great advisors create an environment of trust. They are on your team because you will win together. The stewards of your family's wealth will be focused on helping you reach your Wealth Purpose.

2. **Professional.** Wisdom results when the collaboration from multiple professional stakeholders is interspersed into your decision-making process. Finding the right help in building your Wealth Purpose is important; finding help that is collaborative, and not divisive, is critical. People don't need to always agree – in fact, when they don't, you often get the best of the 360 degree approach you want – but contrarians or spoilers can compromise the plan.

3. **Empathetic.** Some of the most difficult financial decisions happen when things change: when there is a devastating illness or death; divorce or major blindspots to the plan. Stewards of your Wealth Plan will help you to grow, clarify your values, reposition your Wealth Plan as required, moderate in difficult family or business situations and provide you with the leadership skills you need to keep focused in times of change. In short, they will be focused on helping you reach your maximum Wealth Potential.

Consider the following process for finding and selecting your financial team:

1. Write down your top three tax and investment questions.

2. Google them, and get the best answers the internet can provide, for context.

3. Ask for referrals to the top people in the area of specialization you seek help with.

4. Look for an independent practitioner, as well as one who works for a firm, for a comparison of services, fees, and communication styles.

5. Make an appointment and interview the candidates.

6. Rate the advisors using the following guide:

Choosing Financial Professionals: Who will advise me on achieving my Tax-Efficient Wealth Purpose?

Criteria	My Notes	Points *
Educator		
Probes and clarifies my objectives		
Answers my questions		
Clarifies terms		
Ensures I understand		
Suggests a process		
Advocate		
Is strategic – long term thinker		
Explains risks		
Has access to resources		
Has recent qualifications or updating education		
Displays wisdom and experience		
Steward		
Fee transparency – what will I pay, when, what's included in the fee		
Demonstrates care with my money		
Ready to moderate in difficult situations		
Can help me refine my Life and Wealth Purpose		

* Great: 3 points, Good: 1 point. Inadequate: 0 points. Max. Potential: 14 x 3 = 42 points

Now choose your key advisor and establish principles for a close working relationship.

The Money Moral

Get the Right Help. While you shouldn't abdicate responsibility for your Wealth Purpose to anyone else, you don't have to do this alone. Look for professionals who will work for you in ensuring that your long term strategy is sound and that you are fully compliant with all regulation. Never compromise on strategy or compliance in your process.

NOTE: *My Top Three Tax and Investment Questions*

MANAGE BEHAVIOURAL FINANCE:
SLAY TAX DRAGONS

Building a Wealth Purpose is an important commitment. You've got your number: the definitive goal that describes financial freedom for you; and you have embarked on a financial journey with your most trusted advisors. It's one that will face a series of risks; an important reason why you will build "tax homes" for shelter. And it will require a strategy for the implementation of a multi-stakeholder approach within your family, too.

Wealth is only meaningful if it is sustainable over time, and ultimately, if it can be shared. A Family Wealth Purpose is much more powerful, even if you are single today.

Achieving your Wealth Purpose will, in fact, require collaboration with a family team that can include your parents, siblings, spouse and children or in the rare instance where you are the last one, the community at large to whom you will ultimately leave your remaining wealth.

By its very nature, a multi-stakeholder approach to anything brings a complexity that needs to be controlled and managed. Therefore, you need to anticipate the variety of behavioural risks others bring to your ultimate wealth accumulations. Certainly complacency and disinterest are amongst the biggest; you have already overcome these personally by deciding to read these pages.

Complacency and disinterest by advisors or other family members can make the achievement and sustainability of your ultimate Wealth Purpose more difficult. So can financial infidelity: when individuals fall out of line with the commitment to the Wealth Purpose to pursue self-interests.

Family wealth management requires that everyone is on the same page – lawyers, accountants, investment advisors, business valuators, insurance specialists and so on, with all the participants to the plan and therefore is somewhat self-regulating. Having one trusted advisor who works as your "general manager" of the entire team helps, because that person will drive the strategy, the process and the plan. It doesn't really matter which of the professionals takes this role; what's important is that this person is fully committed to executing on your plan.

Likewise, the best Tax Strategies that accompany and complement your Wealth Purpose implement family income splitting and asset management techniques that deliver overall lower taxes payable for the group. Bringing the family together as a whole, when preparing tax returns and planning "tax homes" for every dollar to be invested, brings better wealth results, faster. In short,

> *Your family becomes a more powerful economic unit when you make tax efficient wealth management decisions together.*

Therefore, behavioural finance is an important concept in family wealth management. Some of the more expensive financial consequences of behavioural finance include unaddressed issues under three main categories. You will want to anticipate these and have a plan to address them:

1. **Control.** Wealth management suffers when families don't have systems in place for wealth transfers from one generation to the next. Sound tax planning strategies will address the right time for asset transfers – during your lifetime, for example, or at death. Both older and younger generations need a way to discuss this and then, put into place the legal documentation to direct the required results. This includes living wills, powers of attorney and wills. You'll need the help of a lawyer to draft these documents, but an experienced tax specialist to drive the process. Many families avoid this subject entirely, at the great peril of the financial legacy. A tax specialist will address the issues annually as a part of their professional process. Finding that specialist therefore is important. *Doing so at your weakest moment; when you are sick or disabled, is not as successful as planning for your most powerful financial moments.*

2. **Competence.** Not everyone is equally good with money. That's why most families defer to a "Chief Financial Officer." That's the

person who tends to take responsibility for the budgets, the investments and the tax returns. If you are that trusted leader, it's incumbent upon you to set and share the strategy, principles and process in place to manage intergenerational wealth. No matter how well you do as an individual, the burden of wealth includes instructions for the next generation and the stewardship that comes with guiding required outcomes. If you fail to set that up that path, and teach the financial principles for the preservation of wealth, your financial legacy will fail. You, in other words, become responsible not only for the Wealth Purpose on behalf of the group, but also for ensuring that complacency and disinterest will not upset the plan.

3. **Conflict.** It's unavoidable, but manageable. Siblings fight, marriages dissolve, business partners fall out. Make sure you anticipate financial outcomes in times of conflict – when you still like each other. Prenuptial agreements, buy-sell agreements, wills, powers of attorney and guidelines for effective communications in stressful times, like business failure, job loss, illness and death, preserve both dignity and wealth. If you have a Wealth Purpose, you will put these in place. Also, it's important to draw financial boundaries. Business partners who don't follow the business plan require a process for getting back on track; the same is true of participants in your family's Wealth Purpose. Wise and effective leaders will establish the negotiables and the non-negotiables to the plan.

No matter how old you are today, take the time to determine who the stakeholders to your Wealth Plan are. On the professional side they may be tax accountants, legal advisors, financial planners, insurance specialists or business valuators. But on the personal side, they could be parents, spouses, children, siblings, employees, the community. If you are going to be in the centre of a multi-stakeholder plan – which you will if you have a family – it's important to have everyone on the same page when it comes to your long term strategic plan for tax efficient wealth accumulation.

You'll have to put some work into financial literacy and understanding investing principles. But to accumulate, grow, preserve and transition sustainable wealth, for your own enjoyment and to future generations, you will need to lead in the area of tax literacy. Here are the four most common "tax dragons" to slay:

1. **The Moving Target Obstacle**. Tax rules change every year with federal and provincial budgets. It's tough to master a moving target, let alone two: in some years, your life can change faster than the tax laws. At the same time, it's important to keep up with the very subject you and your family may not understand well at all. Find a good source of interpretive tax news and keep up with the changes. Try *Knowledge Bureau Report*; the daily financial news, and the information available through your government and financial institutions.

2. **The Documentation Obstacle**. The Canada Revenue Agency (CRA) has been a major driver of technology in its communications with taxpayers. Over 80% of all tax returns filed by Canadians are transmitted electronically now. Ever-changing technology is a problem for some: how do you "think taxes first" when you carry your whole financial life in your hip pocket and all your financial transactions are electronic? The "shoebox" of receipts is so "last century," isn't it? In a world in which people deposit cheques by taking pictures of them, receipt-keeping likewise requires a proper set of electronic drawers. Because tax efficiency requires inter-family collaboration to maximize tax filing and investment transactions, every stakeholder must be committed to keeping documentation and filing their taxes every year and on time.

3. **The Ostrich Approach**. CRA makes millions of dollars on people who file tax returns late. It's a real waste of financial resources. Everyone in the family will need to buy in, especially your spouse, whose tax debt can become your problem. Electronic filing seems very simple and invisible, but, you still have to meet a hard deadline: file your tax return by April 30 to avoid late filing and/or interest penalties, or gross negligence, which is 50% of the taxes you owe and avoided paying. Unincorporated business owners have until June 15; but will pay interest on balances due if payment is not received by April 30.

4. **The Fear Factor**. While things have evolved with technology, some things never change. Tax audits are the biggest, scariest obstacle of all for most people and with good reason: auditors have real power to invoke penalties that will significantly reduce your wealth. You cannot circumvent the intent of the law in your tax planning activities, nor can you evade taxes. Tax evasion evokes the BIG penalties. If you choose to deliberately overstate tax

deductions and credits or understate income you will pay up to 200% of the taxes evaded (and/or go to jail in severe cases). It is one risk to your Wealth Purpose you and any of the stakeholders to your plan will want to avoid, period.

The Money Moral

Surround yourself with the best people – professionals and family stakeholders to help you build your Wealth Purpose. In a family setting, it's important that everyone is on the same page.

NOTES: *Who are the family stakeholders to my Wealth Purpose?*

_____

_____

_____

_____

Who is the Chief Financial Officer?

_____

_____

_____

THE MONEY MORALS:
DEFINE YOUR WEALTH PURPOSE

Have a Wealth Purpose. It may be tougher in the future to meet your financial goals and manage emerging risks without deliberate financial goals. Fortunately, those with a Wealth Purpose will do extremely well as global wealth trends indicate.

Add a Tax Strategy. Own your Wealth Purpose, and the glue that holds your choices together – your Tax Strategy. Those who add tax efficiency to the mix can achieve their Wealth Purpose more quickly.

Get the Right Help. While you shouldn't abdicate responsibility for your Wealth Purpose to anyone else, you don't have to do this alone. Look for professionals who will work for you in ensuring your long term strategy is sound and that you are fully compliant with all regulations. Never compromise on strategy or compliance.

Manage Financial Behaviors. Surround yourself with the best people – professionals and family stakeholders – to help you build your Wealth Purpose. In a family setting, it's important that everyone is on the same page.

Follow Six Steps to Your Wealth Purpose:

1. **STRATEGIZE** – Create Your Wealth Plan

2. **COMPLY** – Get Expert Tax Help

3. **CONSUME** – With Low-Taxed Dollars

4. **SAVE** – With Tax Assistance

5. **GROW** – Manage Your Money Buckets

6. **PRESERVE** – Live Your Wealth Purpose!

Process Charts: Create Your Wealth Plan

1. HOW MUCH IS ENOUGH?

One Year	3 Years	5 Years	10 Years	20 Years	30 Years	40 Years
$	$	$	$	$	$	$

2. WHERE DO YOU STAND NOW?

		NOW	3 YEARS	5 YEARS
ASSETS	**DESCRIPTION**	**$**	**$**	**$**
Cash	Non-interest bearing			
Short Term Investments	In non-registered accounts: Interest-bearing Accounts T-Bills, Money Market, Other Debt Instruments			
Cash Surrender Values	Life Insurance Policies			
Financial Assets – Long Term Investments	Pensions: Employer Funded RPP and/or DPSP			
	Pensions: Private – RRSP, RRIF, Annuities			
	Non-Registered: Stocks, Bonds, Mutual Funds,			
	Tax Free Savings Accounts (TFSAs)			
Non-Financial Assets	Real Estate: Personal Residence			
	Real Estate: Vacation Properties, Rental Properties			
	Business Assets			
Other Personal Assets	Art, Antiques, Furnishing Vehicles, Boats, Other			
	Total Assets			
LIABILITIES				
Short Term Obligations	Lines of Credit, Credit Cards, Income Taxes			
Short Term Loans	Home Mortgage, Car Loans, Demand Notes, etc.			
Long Term Investment Loans	Deductible Mortgages, Investment Loans, etc.			
	Total Liabilities			
Assets - Liabilities =	**Personal Net Worth**			

PART 2 – COMPLY

Meet Chet and Catherine...

Chet can't remember not being in love with Catherine. They met at a dance at the lake quite by chance. Chet's family had always had a cottage at Rainbow Falls; Catherine's family struggled to get by as they were newcomers to Canada over 20 years ago. She was staying with a girlfriend for a week at the lake as a special treat her usually overly-protective parents allowed, after her stellar scholastic achievements.

Catherine was their great pride. The eldest daughter of four offspring, she was named after a heroine in a book her pregnant mom was reading as they travelled over to a new life in Canada. Catherine was smart, articulate, a born leader. Her parents were somewhat dismayed initially, when she fell in love with the personable Chet at the tender age of 16 on that fateful visit to Rainbow Falls. But she was studious, she worked hard at her after-school job and she won a number of scholarships that enabled her to go to university. Now here she was, a radiant bride-to-be at the age of 22, with a year left before graduation from her master's program in speech pathology.

Chet was outstanding too. The captain of the football team, the winner of a football scholarship and a first draft choice to a coveted internship at the oldest and most prestigious legal firm in the province, Chet's future was very bright. At 26, he was ready to take on the world. He had already saved enough money to buy a home with a substantial down payment and in his new role at the Firm, it seemed that this was the right time to begin his journey with the love of his life.

For the first time, Chet realized that his Wealth Purpose was about to change. With his upcoming marriage, his new, stronger economic unit would include Catherine and a lot of tax questions. Let's listen in...

SIMPLE TAX RULES FOR
KEEPING MORE

Chet Learns Money Morals from his Dad, Thomas

There's a reason why those who have more, care more about taxes. This is a lesson Chet learned early from his father, Thomas, a financial advisor with one of the big banks. Chet was immersed in financial literacy, from a young age.

Thomas was adamant that his son should learn commercial math skills; non-negotiable were sharp recall skills in the basic math functions – addition, subtraction, multiplication and division. As a child, Chet would listen, fascinated, to his dad explain how fractions turned into decimals and how to use each to analyze various circumstances; like fixed and variable costs involved with his summer lemonade stand, for example, which to this day forms part of the neighborhood folklore.

The two of them would practice every morning at breakfast, with all the skills coming together in one long division question – different every day. Young Chet took his time with his "g'sintas." "Six g'sinta 72 how many times, dad?" he would holler up the stairs, on the days he beat his dad to the breakfast table. Chet carefully subtracted, added, subtracted again and proudly placed decimals, as required. Proud dad, Thomas, joked that doing division long-hand was a better mind sharpener than coffee was. To this day, at the age of 58, he still solves a division problem or two, longhand, every morning.

Chet would learn to understand other important concepts, like pro-ration, for example. His father had a home office and he explained to his son that for tax purposes, he had to separate out the area used for business purposes and prorate all the household expenses to take out the business components from the personal components. They would sit down once a month on Sundays to sort through the bills, pay them and ready them for the bookkeeper; who was in charge of satisfying the Taxman his dad would say, peering over his reading specs. Chet did the proration to determine what percentage of all the home expenses would be used as a deduction against his father's income; to his father's overall approval.

(He would never admit this to his dad, but Chet pictured the Taxman to be a mysterious guy with no first name – in a black hat and trench coat and a deep booming voice; a bit of a scary figure.)

Thomas also taught Chet about the **time value of money.**

A dollar in your own pocket today is worth more than a dollar you will have in the future, provided it has the potential to earn investment income for you.

Young people can really benefit from the time value of money, he would tell Chet. The more money you save immediately, the better you can take advantage of the compounding of your investment income.

"What's compounding, Dad?" Chet asked. "Google it!" Came the reply.

"It looks like it's interest earned on your interest," said Chet. "So, if I keep investing the interest I earn on my investments, my bigger balance will earn even more!" The boy was quick.

"The Taxman uses the time value of money to his own advantage," Chet's dad would point out next. "He takes a percentage of the first dollars employees earn – before they even see the money for them-selves – to fund social programs and pay for the costs of running government." The two had a fairly detailed conversation about the role of the CRA – Canada Revenue Agency – and how it not only col-lected tax on behalf of the federal and provincial governments, but also redistributed those tax dollars to lower-income earners.

Thomas explained that every resident of Canada was required to report income earned from around the world in Canadian dollars every year on the T1 General *Income and Benefits Return*, which he took the time to print for his son, so he could see it. "Wow, lots of words I don't understand here," said Chet.

"That's true of most adults," Thomas chuckled at his son, "but we have to understand this, because it is our legal right and duty to arrange our financial affairs to pay the correct amount of tax, but no more. And because there is some discretion in how we earn income – actively or passively – we can plan to minimize the taxes we have to pay."

As Chet grew older, he had a firm grasp on why paying taxes under our "*self-assessment*" system of taxation made sense in society. He also came to learn a series of principles his father used over the years in complying with the requirements of the Taxman – which seemed to change constantly – and at the same time, increase the savings he had for the family.

Thomas had three key principles that governed his financial decision-making:

1. **Keep more of the first dollars earned** and invest them, as soon as you can.

2. **Hold onto your investments** over several years, if possible, in tax-free or tax deferred investment accounts to their maximum allowable limits.

3. **Make sure your resulting money has purchasing power** when you need it. This meant, in practice, that Chet and his father were on the look-out for investment returns that beat the rate of inflation, taxes payable on the earnings and the investment fees payable.

Thomas shared other financial wisdoms with his son. Canada's taxation system is a "*progressive*" one; he explained. That is: *the more you earn the more you pay.* He illustrated this with a chart of current tax brackets and rates and explained that generally the brackets changed annually with an indexing factor to take the cost of living into account:

Federal Tax Brackets and Tax Rates

2016 Brackets	Rates
Up to $11,474	0
$11,475 to $45,282	15%
$45,282 to $90,563	20.5%*
$90,564 to $140,388	26%
$140,389 to $200,000	29%
Over $200,000	33%

*The 22% tax bracket is expected to drop to 20.5% once the newly elected government of 2015 delivers its Budget. A 33% bracket is also expected on income over $200,000. Brackets are estimated based on CPI rates.

He went on to give a simplistic example of how tax brackets and rates work. Four adults earning $11,000 each would make $44,000 in total for the family unit and pay no tax, Thomas explained. But one person making $44,000[1] would give the federal government about $4,300. That person would also pay to the provincial government, approximately $2,150 for a total of $6,450, assuming he or she was single. That would leave you with just over $37,500 to spend and invest – about $500 a month less than the efforts of the four people individually.

Chet found this quite amazing. First, that this single person would give up an average of 15% of his earnings right away for tax purposes, and second that there was such economic advantages when families thought of their finances as a household.

Family income splitting is, therefore, an important principle in family wealth management.

His father concurred with Chet's conclusion. "This is an important first principle to understand within a progressive tax system. Because of the obvious advantages, family income splitting is subject to special rules that essentially block the ability for higher earners to transfer income and assets to lower earners in the family."

"It would seem to be too good to be true, Dad," Chet sighed with a hint of young cynicism.

Thomas smiled. "There are some legitimate ways to get around these **'Attribution Rules'**, son." Chet noted the new term and the important thought: tax planning as a family unit is an important strategy in

[1] 2015 tax rates

funding financial milestones like education, retirement and potential incapacity.

"As well, you should know that different income sources attract different tax rates," Thomas informed his son, who raised one eyebrow in curiosity to think about that concept:

When multiple income sources are earned by
several taxpayers in the family, instead of just one,
the household together can successfully average
taxes downward, for all individuals in the family.

There was one more thing Thomas wanted to add. Chet's head was starting to spin a bit. "Canadians are taxed on worldwide income in their province of residence as of December 31 of the tax year. This can make a big difference in how much you pay," Thomas told his son. "You will want to plan residence moves to a low-taxed province before the end of the tax year; and it would seem obvious, to a high taxed province at the start of the year."

It was time to call it a night.

The Money Moral

Understanding Canada's progressive tax system and its effects on family earnings provides for a multitude of planning opportunities. Multiple family members sharing tax burdens do much better, after tax, than singles do.

Quickie Tax Quiz

1. What were Thomas' three financial principles for accumulating wealth?

2. What three action plans did Chet establish to take control of his wealth building activities?

3. What is the time value of money?

Check out the answers in *Family Tax Essentials Portal* at www.knowledgebureau.com.

BE TAX EFFICIENT:
DIVERSIFY INCOME SOURCES

As Chet learned from his father, a buck is not a buck when it comes to taxation. There are, in fact, many definitions of income on the tax return itself – total income, net income, taxable income and earned income. But different types of income can attract different rates of tax. This was new to Chet. He was starting to understand that how you make a buck, and when you make it will ultimately decide how much tax you'll pay on it. Some planning was obviously in order.

But Chet's father taught him something new again as they discussed tax rates and investments the following night after dinner. Chet learned that his Marginal Tax Rate (MTR) could actually be a more enlightening number. It, too, is linked to the tax bracket Chet's income falls into.

"In fact, a taxpayer's MTR is a useful tool in measuring tax-efficiency of both actively and passively earned income sources," Thomas told his son, indulging in yet another new acronym. "It will tell you how much tax you'll pay on the next type of dollar you plan to earn, while measuring the effect of that income on your eligibility for tax credits and social benefits delivered through the tax system."

Chet estimated his total employment income for the year would be $100,000 and when he ran this number through his Income Tax Estimator,[1] he found his total taxes payable (federal and Ontario provincial) would be approximately $26,000; a 26% average tax rate. His

---

[1] See Knowledge Bureau's Income Tax Estimator to try this for yourself. Just logon to your *Family Tax Essentials* online environment.

total taxable income was reduced by a Basic Personal Amount – a tax free zone on the first $11,000 plus[2] income you earn – and then was subject to a progressively higher rate of tax, applied as his income rose through the brackets.

As he played with the tax estimator he discover two basic tax principles:

The more you earn the more you pay, and the less you receive from income-tested tax credits and social benefits.

"That's a double-whammy." Chet's father nodded in agreement.

"To understand this better – how various income sources are taxed – and then, how to manage and control how you choose to earn them, consider that the tax return requires the reporting of four broad categories of income," he said, noting them on a white board in his home-based office:

Ordinary income, which is generally fully taxable and includes income from employment, public and private pensions and interest earned on your investments. It may also include alimony and certain social benefits like Employment Insurance, and net rental income – what's left after allowable deductions from gross rents.

Dividends are the after-tax distribution of profits from private or public Canadian corporations to their shareholders. Reporting here involves an integration of the corporate and personal tax systems, the end result of which is a preferential tax rate on the dividend. The amount reported and the amount of the credit depends on the source of the dividends – those from large public corporations vs. those from corporations that qualify for what's known as the Small Business Deduction.

Capital gains or losses are reported upon the disposition (sale or transfer) of assets the family owns, some of which may be income-producing. Only half those gains, net of losses, are reported on the return. Sometimes, tax on the gains can be avoided when certain properties are donated to charity; gains on other types of properties may qualify for specific exemptions from tax.

Income from self-employment is self-reported and it is the net income – what's left after business revenues are reduced by allowable

---

[2] See Essential Family Tax Facts Appendix for actual amounts.

deductions – that is subject to tax on the personal tax return – the T1. Income from an incorporated business is treated as income of a separate tax filer (the corporation), and reported on a T2 *Corporation Income Tax Return*.

"If you apply some of your math skills, you can see that capital gains are taxed in the most advantageous manner: only 50% of the income is reported. Dividends are next in line; but they require a "gross up" calculation we'll get to another time," he smiled with a wink. "All the other ordinary income sources including employment income, interest, and pensions are less tax-efficient."

By this time, the bride-to-be, Catherine, had joined the discussion. She was fascinated by the concept of proactively planning their income sources to have more control over the wealth they will accumulate together – after tax.

"Because the marginal tax rate can also be computed on the next type of income you earn, it's a powerful tool that can help you think about diversifying your income sources," her future father-in-law told her.

Encouraged by the young couple's interest in their finances, Thomas took the discussion in another direction. He suggested that he would introduce Chet and Catherine to his tax specialist, someone he had a great deal of trust in: Malcolm Reuler.

Malcolm was a an experienced tax professional who was engaged with Thomas in planning personal, family and succession plans with a tax-first viewpoint. About the same age as Thomas, Malcolm would be delighted to be introduced to the young couple.

A week later, they were immediately charmed by his gentle, collaborative manner, which clearly included a sharp technical knowledge, but also, bright eyes that shone in tandem with a crinkled smile and endearing laugh lines. Malcolm was more than happy to pick up this discussion about marginal tax rates.

A chart depicting the marginal tax rates for different income sources appeared literally out of nowhere, with an example for a taxpayer living in Ontario. Malcolm pointed out that annual indexing of tax brackets and federal or provincial budgets will result in changes to review at the start of every tax year:

Taxable Income Range	Ordinary Income	Capital Gains	Small Bus. Corp. Div.	Eligible Div.
Up to $11,327	0%	0%	0%	0%
$11,328 to $40,922	20.05%	10.03%	5.35%	-6.86%
$40,923 to $44,701	24.15%	12.08%	10.19%	-1.20%
$44,701 to $72,064	31.15%	15.58%	18.45%	8.46%
$72,065 to $81,847	32.98%	16.49%	20.61%	10.99%
$81,848 to $84,902	35.39%	17.70%	23.45%	14.31%
$84,903 to $89,401	39.41%	19.70%	28.19%	19.86%
$89,402 to $138,586	43.41%	21.70%	32.91%	25.38%
$138,587 to $150,000	46.41%	23.20%	36.45%	29.52%
$150,001 to $220,000	47.97%	23.98%	38.29%	31.67%
Over $220,000	49.53%	24.76%	40.13%	33.82%

Note: 2015 rates

Chet and Catherine were fascinated. "This makes it much easier to find tax homes for our dollars," they said, almost in tandem.

"Is it possible to earn any tax exempt income?" asked Catherine. "Yes," was the enthusiastic reply. "First there is any income received that is under the Basic Personal Amounts. But in addition, most people don't know that there are over twenty sources of exempt income." He broke them down categories, and pulled out one of his Tax Tip Sheets to deepen Chet and Catherine's knowledge. On this topic, he did want to zero in on seven specific sources of exempt income that might be of particular relevance:

Checklist of Tax Exempt Receipts

1. Capital gains from the sale of a tax exempt principal residence.
2. Inheritances or gifts.
3. Investment income earned within or withdrawn from a Tax-Free Savings Account (TFSA).
4. Life Insurance Policy proceeds.
5. Capital gains on publicly traded shares donated to a registered charity or private foundation, or, after 2016, gains on the sale of real estate or private shares, if the proceeds are donated within 30 days of the disposition.
6. Benefits from accident, disability, sickness or income maintenance plans – but only if premiums are paid by the beneficiary.
7. Windfalls such as lottery or gambling winnings.

"We will discuss each of these in detail as we discuss your future income and investments," said Malcolm, "but if you ever get to Lucky #7, you'll need to buy me lunch, okay?" Catherine and Chet chuckled.

He ended the session with another surprising tax fact that many taxpayers, including Chet and Catherine didn't know:

Benefits paid for in kind – instead of money – must be included on the tax return.

"This can include anything that has a commercial value, such as a bushel of grain in exchange for payment of a trade debt, a gaggle of geese, gold, shares or a variety of services. To record such income receipts requires valuation and this is closely reviewed by the CRA."

At this point, Malcolm provided some unusually stern emphasis for the final lesson for the day: the definition of *Fair Market Value*. (Chet and Catherine quickly became aware that in any conversation with Malcolm a glossary of new tax terms was bound to arise, together with a whole lot of new acronyms. As the communications specialist, Catherine kept the notes on the new tax language).

"Whenever there is an in-kind transaction or whenever ownership of an asset is transferred to another without the exchange of money, the FMV must be determined," Malcolm told them. "It's something that is often the subject of tax disputes in a variety of circumstances, from transferring assets between family members to charitable donation receipting."

This important concept of FMV, therefore, would come up again and again as Chet and Catherine planned their investments, considered what they will give to charity, and received transfers of property from their parents.

"Keep all valuations (appraisals, newspaper clippings, and other indicators of value) in a safe place for tax reporting purposes," said Malcolm, "because the onus of proof is on you." At this point, he peered with purpose over his reading glasses. Catherine took more notes, faster.

Chet decided he was going to write his tax obligations into his calendar every week. He was a fastidious type of person that way. On Friday afternoons, before signing off for the weekend, he would review his online investment and banking activities; file his income and expense receipts and update his auto log. He intended to claim his car expenses this year and he knew that keeping track of business vs. personal driving was a key requirement.

The Money Moral

When you know your marginal tax rate on the next dollars you earn, you can make better choices about your income sources and tax-preferred investments to reduce your effective tax rate on both income and capital. The result – more money for you!

Quickie Tax Quiz

Can you answer the following questions?

1. What's considered income for tax purposes?
2. What income receipts are tax exempt?
3. How are the income sources you earn affected by your marginal tax rates?

Check out the answers in *Family Tax Essentials Portal* at www.knowledgebureau.com.

WHERE THE GOLD IS:
MAXIMIZING TAX DEDUCTIONS AND CREDITS

Chet and Catherine continued to learn more about their tax filing rights and obligations in their next informal meeting with Malcolm. It was becoming a regular thing – coffee on Thursday afternoons before yoga. It was a great way to start a financial life, with tax literacy. This week, the topic was deductions and credits, and here's what Chet and Catherine learned:

"The vast majority of lines on the tax return are made up of deductions and credits," said Malcolm, and that certainly peaked interest from Chet and Catherine, "So if you are going to miss something on your return, it is likely something to your advantage. That's why you'll want to understand the difference between a tax deduction, a non-refundable and a refundable tax credit. You'll also want to keep all the back-up documents for claiming them, because CRA can and will ask for receipts."

In front of the white board in Malcolm's office once more, three headlines appeared: Tax Deductions, Refundable Tax Credits and Non-refundable Tax Credits. Here's how the conversation evolved:

Understanding Tax Deductions. Malcolm explained that all deductions reduce taxable income, but only certain deductions reduce "Net Income" on the T1 return. "Deductions that reduce Net Income can increase your income-tested credits and benefits, so they are lucrative. They are also worth more, the more you earn. Maximizing all the deductions you are entitled to, therefore provides you with a double tax benefit. If large enough, deductions can reduce your marginal tax rate by putting you into a lower tax bracket."

Duly noted: Catherine and Chet glanced in the affirmative at one another.

Next the topic of tax credits was covered, but it proved to be more complex. "There are three types of tax credits, and people often find this confusing," Malcolm acknowledged. "Let's discuss them one at a time."

Federal Refundable Tax Credits. Malcolm wrote notes under each of the two remaining headings. "These credits are usually income-tested, and they are based on the size of your net family income. That essentially means both of your Net Incomes must be added together for the purposes of determining whether you will qualify to receive the credits." He listed several common credits:

1. *The GST/HST Credit* paid quarterly starting at age 19.

2. *Canada Child Tax Benefit* paid monthly, the month after your child's birth until that child reaches age 18.

3. *Working Income Tax Benefit.* A payment that supplements the expenses of working for people coming off social assistance and other low earners.

4. The *Refundable Medical Expenses Supplement.* This credit supports working people with medical expenses.

5. *Refundable Child Fitness Credit.* A new type of refundable tax credit from the federal government, this one is not income tested. The Refundable Child Fitness Credit equals 15% of fees for eligible fitness activities, up to $1,000 or $150 to parents who have their children enrolled in after-school fitness activities.

"You can see how diverse the credits are – helping Canadians receive everything from sales tax support, to support for the costs of raising minor children and re-entry into the job market. Even if you have no income, you may be eligible for some or all of these credits, so always file a tax return," said Malcolm.

Malcolm stressed again that this was why it was so critical to pay attention to Net Income on the tax return. "This line is your ticket to various tax benefits, and it can be reduced with certain deductions like an RRSP contribution or child care expenses."

This was one tax filing detail that would become one of the first Family Tax Essentials Chet and Catherine would learn as they embarked upon their lives together. The Canadian tax system contained lots of support for families – even though it seemed that uncovering and understanding the myriad of options certainly would take a bit of study. Thank goodness for Malcolm, who was ready to take his tax lesson to the next level.

"The last piece of the framework for minimizing income taxes and maximizing your opportunities to tap into refundable credits and social benefits is contained in column #3 here," said Malcolm, pointing at his white board.

TAX DEDUCTIONS	REFUNDABLE TAX CREDITS	NON-REFUNDABLE CREDITS
REDUCE NET INCOME	DEPEND ON SIZE OF NET INCOME	REDUCE TAXES PAYABLE

"Here's what you need to know about non-refundable tax credits," he began. "They're no good to you unless you have taxable income on which you pay federal or provincial taxes. Advocates for low income earners don't like them because they don't help their constituents, but these credits were put into place to limit the benefits provided to high income earners."

He explained that all provinces have their own system of tax credits. Your province of residence is where you resided on December 31 of the tax year. Malcolm reminded the young couple that everyone qualifies for the Basic Personal Amount (BPA) which is just over $11,000 on the federal tax return these days, so long as you lived in Canada for the full year. The provincial equivalents can vary. So can their tax brackets and rates. Fortunately tax software is a big help in sorting out the value of both federal and provincial credits.

"Remember, this is every individual's 'tax-free zone'," said Malcolm. "Other non-refundable tax credits, depending on your circumstances, can be claimed to increase your tax-free zone. They can include amounts that recognize expenses you have incurred to earn employment income, the source deductions you have paid for the source remittances your employer made on your behalf, your costs of attending post-secondary school, the costs of caregiving for medically infirm people, your charitable giving and your medical expenses."

Malcolm offered a chart to explain non-refundable tax credits potentially claimable by Chet and Catherine, indicating that the next federal or provincial governments could, of course, make changes to them.

Federal Non-Refundable Tax Credits

Name of Federal Non-Refundable Tax Credit	Automatically Entered by Software	Receipts Required
Basic Personal Amount	Yes	No
Age Amount	Yes	No
Spousal Amount	Yes	No
Amount for Eligible Dependants (Equivalent-to-Spouse Amount)	Yes	No
Amount for Infirm Dependants age 18 and Over	Yes	No
Amount for CPP Contributions	Yes	No
Amount for EI Premiums	Yes	No
Volunteer Firefighters Amount	No	Yes
Amount for Emergency Services Volunteers	No	Yes
Canada Employment Amount	Yes	No
Public Transit Amount	No	Yes
Children's Arts Amount	No	Yes
Adoption Expenses	No	Yes
Home Buyers' Amount	No	No
Home Accessibility Tax Credit (New in 2015)	No	Yes
Pension Income Amount	Yes	Yes (slips)
Caregiver Amount	Yes	No
Disability Amount (self or dependant)	No	Yes (T2201)
Interest Paid on Student Loans	No	Yes
Tuition, Education and Textbook Amount (self or dependant)	No	Yes
Medical Expenses	No	Yes
Charitable Donations	No	Yes

Malcolm reminded the couple again that provinces have their own tax credit systems and they don't necessarily all follow the federal credits... another layer of complexity, but a good one, which can reduce taxes payable.

The Money Moral

Pay attention to the tax deductions and tax credits – both refundable and non-refundable ones – that you and your family may qualify for. They create real dollars, sometimes sent to you year round, and they can be leveraged with tax-smart investing.

Quickie Tax Quiz

1. What's the difference between a tax deduction and a tax credit?

2. What's the difference between a refundable tax credit and a non-refundable tax credit?

3. Which non-refundable credits can be claimed without receipts?

   Check out the answers in *Family Tax Essentials Portal* at www.knowledgebureau.com.

NECESSARY EVILS:
TAX FILINGS AND BIG STICKS

"I like to work out my taxes before the end of every tax year, and to do some year-end tax planning," Thomas told Chet after Thanksgiving dinner. "That's why the door is closed to my home office – it's a bit of a paper mess in there." While the rest of the family was enthusiastically arguing over the latest round of Scrabble, father and son retired to the den with their coffees.

"I remember being somewhat shocked to find a balance due rather than a refund when I filed my taxes one year before you were born, son," Thomas chuckled. He had an endearing way of peering over his glasses. "I am sure it was the reason I decided to dedicate my career to the financial services. I hated this surprise and I really thought someone should have told me more about the many things that can be done at year end to avoid it."

Thomas went on to explain how he had to scramble to pay the unexpected bill, and to make it priority one because failure to pay – or to file a tax return too quickly without proper care and accuracy – was so expensive. He worked an extra couple of shifts at the manufacturing plant in town to come up with the money. He also knew that CRA would take payments over time, but he wanted to avoid the interest charges that would be compounding daily on the outstanding amount, back then at an exorbitant rate of 9%. Paying off the balance due quickly was smart money management.

Thankfully, Thomas always filed accurate tax returns, on time. He had a colleague who was a professional tax advisor – Malcolm – and together they worked with clients on building tax efficient wealth for the long term. Malcolm would advise on the taxes payable by expertly computing the tax effects of financial decision-making; Thomas would advise these same clients on the right investment strategies to meet their goals. It was a great way to provide a holistic financial service.

But they both occasionally came in contact with people who didn't voluntarily comply with the *Income Tax Act* and, as a result, faced a myriad of big penalties for turning a blind eye to the law.

"Gross negligence penalties of 50% of taxes owing can be added to your tax bill," Thomas told his son, "if you are willfully inattentive to our complex tax laws. That's why it's important to use the services of a professional who has kept up to date with tax changes, if you can't find the time to do it yourself. Aside from gross negligence penalties, those who file their taxes late face more fines:

- 5% of amounts owing plus 1% per month for up to 12 months.

- 10% of amounts owing plus 2% per month for up to 20 months if you were charged a late filing penalty in any of the preceding three tax years."

Chet already knew that taxpayers who participate in tax evasion will face even more penalties by being charged with an offense. When a taxpayer is guilty of an offense, a criminal prosecution takes place. While in the case of gross negligence, the burden of proof is on the taxpayer; in tax evasion cases, the burden is on CRA to show that there was willful intent to understate income or overstate deductions and credits and that there is no reasonable doubt of the crime.

Chet had not been aware of this and took note to research more recent tax cases once he got back into the office on Tuesday. He found that those convicted of tax evasion face a series of penalties, the most common of which is a fine – not less than 100% and not more than 200% of the tax sought to be evaded or credits sought to be gained. Wow – very expensive indeed!

But there was more: this tax evasion penalty could also be accompanied by a prison term of not more than five years. All of this was in addition to the administrative penalties CRA can charge – gross negligence, late filing, and interest compounded daily.

Always be sure to file your return before midnight April 30[1] to avoid late filing penalties. Then if you owe, pay the bill promptly to avoid and expensive interest charges. Do know that you can voluntarily comply with the law to correct errors or omissions you may have made. If you do so before CRA finds you negligent, you will avoid penalties and interest and, in severe cases of fraud, jail.

Quickie Tax Quiz

1. What fines may be levied for filing late?
2. What is the amount of a gross negligence penalty?
3. Where is the burden of proof in tax evasion cases?

   Check out the answers in *Family Tax Essentials Portal* at www.knowledgebureau.com.

---

[1] Or the following Monday if April 30 falls on a weekend.

TAX RECORDS IN
HIP POCKETS

"You seem to be glad to have our first tax season behind us!" Chet smiled at his bride-to-be. Catherine was doing her best to clean up her apartment before moving at the end of the month in anticipation of their May wedding. She was throwing out the paperwork she didn't need and her tax records were at the top of her list.

"Don't be so quick dispose of your tax files," her fiance wisely counseled, "you will need to keep them in case of audit."

Catherine frowned. "Just how long do I need to keep them?" Chet had been reading up on this. "All records and all vouchers necessary to verify the information must be kept until *six years after the end of the taxation year* to which those records relate."

"Speak English, please," Catherine frowned as shrugged her shoulders, not comprehending.

"Well, this year's tax receipts must be kept six years after the end of this calendar year."

Now Catherine's mouth fell open. "Really? We have to carry these boxes with us for all that time?"

"'Fraid so, sweety," came the reply. "Catherine, you should also know as a self-employed person, your burden is somewhat greater. It looks like you need to keep any books and records to enable CRA to determine the amount of taxes payable – that covers a pretty wide swath – and they expect them to be kept in proper order. We'll have to make sure this stuff is easily retrievable for your future sanity and our pocketbook!"

"Exactly what is a 'record' for tax purposes anyway, now that we all live in an electronic world?" Catherine wanted to know. "That's a good question for Malcolm," said Chet and so it was on the next visit to the kindly man that the question came up. His answer was complete, as usual, as he interpreted the rules:

"Well, a 'record' includes a host of things: an account, an agreement, a book, a chart or table, a diagram, a form, an image, an invoice, a letter, a map, a memorandum, a plan, a return, a statement, a telegram" (really? – even Malcolm smirked at this), "and any other thing containing information, whether in writing or in any other form...get the picture?" he asked. Chet and Catherine nodded.

"If you're self-employed, you'll need to keep sales invoices, purchase invoices, cash register receipts, formal written contracts, credit card receipts, delivery slips, deposit slips, work orders, dockets, cheques, bank statements, your tax returns, and your general correspondence."

"So...I thought CRA was big on electronic filing! This sounds like this will involve renting a storage locker!" Catherine exclaimed. Malcolm agreed. "But, the good news is that paper source documents may be disposed if you keep good electronic images as your permanent records. Recordkeeping, quite literally is now a snap – as more people take pictures of their receipts and store them electronically."

"What happens if your records are, well, sketchy?" asked Chet. The reply was straight forward: "In that case, CRA can specify what records and books of account they want and if you fail to comply with this request, you can be fined. As usual, this is expensive. The maximum penalties in fact break down into potential types:

- a fine of not less than $1,000 and not more than $25,000

- both a fine and imprisonment for up to 12 months.

If you decide to destroy or dispose of your records to evade the payment of tax you'll be in a lot more trouble: you will be prosecuted for tax evasion."

"What if I want to get rid of these records sooner than the six-year required retention period – let's say we move, for example?" asked Catherine. Again the answer was clear, although not one that either Catherine, Chet or Malcolm preferred:

"You must first request permission to destroy records before the six-year required period is up, and file a special Form T137 *Request for Destruction of Records*. But, know that this is generally not a good idea – it's a direct invitation for CRA to verify your records in a full audit prior to destruction."

The Money Moral

Keep your books and records to justify the numbers on your tax returns for a minimum retention period of six years after the end of the taxation year to which those records relate and make sure they are in good order and that you can find them if CRA wants to see them.

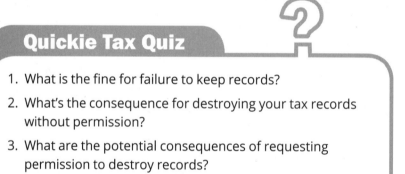

Quickie Tax Quiz

1. What is the fine for failure to keep records?
2. What's the consequence for destroying your tax records without permission?
3. What are the potential consequences of requesting permission to destroy records?

   Check out the answers in *Family Tax Essentials Portal* at www.knowledgebureau.com.

THE MONEY MORALS:
COMPLY WITH EXPERTISE

1. **In Canada, Taxpayers File as Individuals.** Understanding Canada's progressive tax system and its effects on family earnings provides for a multitude of planning opportunities. Each individual is taxed at progressively higher rates as earnings rise. Multiple family members sharing tax burdens do much better, after tax, than singles do; everyone benefits from the Basic Personal Amount and tax brackets that account for rises in taxable income.

2. **Know Your Marginal Tax Rate on Different Income Sources.** When you know your marginal tax rate on the next dollars you earn, you can make better choices about your income sources and tax-preferred investments to reduce the overall tax rate you'll pay on both income and capital. The result – more money for you!

3. **Really Dig for Tax Deductions and Credits that Reduce Your Income.** Pay attention to the tax deductions and tax credits – both refundable and non-refundable ones – that you and your family may qualify for. They create real dollars – sometimes sent to you year round – and they can be leveraged with tax-smart investing.

4. **File and Pay on Time.** Always be sure to file your return before midnight April 30 to avoid late filing penalties. Then if you owe, pay the bill promptly to avoid and expensive interest charges. Do know that you can voluntarily comply with the law to correct errors or omissions you may have made. If you do so before CRA finds you negligent, you will avoid penalties and interest and, in severe cases of fraud, jail.

5. **Record Retention is for Six Years.** Keep your books and records to justify the numbers on your tax returns for a minimum retention period of six years after the end of the taxation year to which those records relate and make sure they are in good order and that you can find them if CRA wants to see them.

PROCESS CHART:
Integrate Tax Filing Milestones & Obligations

January: • Jan 2: reduce your tax withholdings at source: file your TD1 form to claim tax credits and a T1213 form • Make your annual TFSA deposit • Jan 30: Interest payment on inter-spousal loans	July: • Investors: Do a Portfolio review • Businesses: business valuation • Retirees: Review RRSP meltdown strategies • Fall Instalment payment review • Real Estate: Cottage/Home Valuations
February: • Feb 28: T4, T5 slips due • Federal Budget review (dates vary)	August: • Back to school expense planning review • File for WITB prepayment
March: • March 2: RRSP filing deadline • March 16: PAR deadline • March 15: Quarterly tax instalment due • March 31: T3 slips due • March 31: File T1-OVP if applicable	September: • Sept. 15: Quarterly instalment due • Cash Flow & Debt Management Review • Risk Management: Insurance Review • Review: Postponement of OAS • Education Funding: Invest CCTB, RESP
April: • April 15 US Tax filing, Form 8938, 4868 • April 30 T1 individual tax filing deadline • Form T1135, even if not filing a tax return • T1ADJ – Late elections for pension income splitting for 2012 expire April 30, 2016	October: • Oct. 15 US Tax filing (if Form 4868 extension of filing time filed) • Review family income splitting • Inter-spousal loan planning
May: • Will and estate planning review	November: • CSB, CPB, investment portfolio review
June: • June 15 T1 proprietorship filing deadline • June 15 quarterly instalment • June 15 Closer Connection Exception Statement for Aliens (IRS Form 8840) • June 30 – File RC243 TFSA Return if applicable • June 30 – File RC312E – Reportable Transactions	December: • RESP, RDSP investments • Tax loss selling • Strategic philanthropy • Dec. 15/31 instalments • Opt out of CPP – Form CPT30

PART 3 – CONSUME

WITH YOUR
TAX REFUNDS

Chet and Catherine were starting to understand that there is a distinct difference between tax planning and tax preparation. They go hand in hand of course, but most people pay taxes first and then try to plan later.

Chet and Catherine knew that by turning that paradigm around – by planning their after-tax results first and then paying taxes accordingly – they would build more wealth, more quickly than the vast majority of Canadians.

Most people they knew, in fact, could not tell them that the tax filing deadline is April 30 for individual taxpayers. Yet everyone seemed to know that filing for a tax refund is an important milestone, and that they usually got one!

With the average tax refund coming in at about $1700, or the equivalent of about $142 a month, there is a significant value proposition when tax and financial advisors get together to discuss how to best use this money. The one big question that needs to be discussed is this:

"Are you going to spend it, invest it or pay off debt?"

Chet and Caroline liked their tax advisor, Malcolm, and trusted him. He was a true financial educator to them, willing to meet at the drop of a hat. But he was also an advocate for their smooth relationship with the CRA and in stewarding their money through various tax obstacles. He was an experienced practitioner who had helped many families in their town. He also was on a personal mission to help young couples like this one really understand their options when it comes to tax-efficient investing.

When their friends asked them what to look for in a professional tax advisor, that's what they would reply: "Look for someone who is a financial educator, an advocate for you when you have a financial problem and a steward of your future resources."

Malcolm had discussed six strategies for building wealth using a tax refund. He drew them up on the whiteboard after their tax returns were filed:

Six Smart Things to Do with Your Refund

✓ Pay Off Debt

✓ TFSA

✓ RRSP

✓ Home Ownership

✓ Insurance

✓ Other Accounts

Malcolm's commentary was characteristically short and sweet:

1. **Pay off Non-Deductible Debt.** Malcolm didn't seem to mind deductible debt so much. But expensive, non-deductible debt, like credit card balances, seemed to really aggravate him. Pay them off first, he would say... then vow to budget and live within your means, saving first, before spending. *If you must borrow money or pay fees, make sure they're tax deductible.*

2. **Invest in a TFSA** – The Tax Free Savings Account. It's such a big gift to young people in particular. Malcolm always radiated complete awe when he spoke about the TFSA. "It's such a great place to park money and earn tax free investment income. *Disciplined savings here will make each of you a millionaire by the time you retire.*"

3. **Use Available RRSP Room.** If there is taxable income, investing in an RRSP brings immediate tax savings with a tax deduction. Depending on your marginal tax rate, the tax savings are in the double-digits – money that can then be used for a TFSA contribution, Malcolm explained.

   "The RRSP is meant for retirement savings. But you can also tap into the funds tax free to fund a home purchase under a special feature called the *Home Buyers' Plan* or, if you wish, you can fund a return to school under the *Lifelong Learning Plan*. It's a tax free loan from your RRSP, as long as you follow up with a repayment plan."

A strategy to save equally in the RRSP as a couple is important, Malcolm pointed out, even in times in your life when one of you is not working; for example to have children or provide elder care. *A spousal RRSP – whereby the higher earner contributes to a lower earner's RRSP but takes the deduction in the higher earner's return – can help equalize taxable pension income withdrawals.*

4. **Invest in a Principal Residence**. When the equity in your home grows, the gains you make are tax exempt. That's true for one principal residence per family, so that is a good investment for a young couple. Malcolm noted that Chet had already invested in a home. "What's critical is to take on only manageable debt. Your dream home is something you may wish to build up to, using your tax exempt gains from the sale of your current home, to fund the next one," he advised.

5. **Insurance**. "While insurance premiums are paid for with after-tax dollars; that is, there is no deduction for the premiums, they are less expensive when you're younger and healthy," said Malcolm. "The RRSP is for you, but this investment is for your heirs: a completely tax exempt benefit that's payable almost immediately after death. Buying the right amount of life insurance is a great way to ensure funding your children's education or paying off the debt on your mortgage. In other words, you are managing the risk of losing your earning power. You will need to budget for this and, if possible, supplement your private coverage with group coverage at work."

6. **Invest in Other Non-Registered Savings Accounts.** "If you have done all of the above, you might just want to park your refund in a non-registered account to earn tax efficient income like dividends and capital gains." Malcolm put down his marker at this point in the meeting and chuckled.

"Yes it's true, despite my best advice and intentions, some of my clients simply succumb to the pleasure of consumerism when they get that large tax refund deposited," He winked. "Oh well, at least it stimulates the economy!"

Chet and Catherine smiled back, each thinking about the wedding that would soon take place and how hard it will be to save in any one of the right places – or at all – at least this year. They understood that finding a tax efficient home for their tax refund would make it grow.

Malcolm, in the meantime, was busy drawing what looked roughly like a house on the white board. Chet and Catherine smiled at one another. Their accountant was either boasting new-age art skills, or proving that he was best to stick to numbers! What followed was fascinating.

The Money Moral

A big tax refund is a bad thing, especially if you could be using the money to grow for you in an appropriate tax home all year long, rather than waiting until several months after the calendar year end for a repayment of the interest-free loan you gave to the government. Be sure you pay only the correct amount of tax, no more, all year long.

Quickie Tax Quiz

1. Why is a tax refund a bad thing?

2. What options are available for the use of RRSP savings without jeopardizing retirement income?

3. What are six great things a taxpayer can do with a tax refund?

   Check out the answers in *Family Tax Essentials Portal* at www.knowledgebureau.com.

GIVE EVERY DOLLAR
A TAX HOME

"Research tells us that educated people who engage in comprehensive financial planning feel more confident about their future"[1], Malcolm turned from the white board to face Chet and Catherine.

"It dismays me, but, financial plans often have significant gaps – they simply are not finished – if they are not prepared in consultation with your team of experts: financial advisors, tax advisors, insurance advisors and legal advisors," he said.

Catherine cocked her head to one side. She was not sure she understood. She was worried about paying down debt on their new home and next month's credit card bills; certainly she didn't need a comprehensive financial plan for that. It was pretty clear she would have to watch her own cash flow carefully (and perhaps get a weekend job to buy the fantasy designer shoes she drooled over on the way to work this morning. Catherine hadn't told her future husband about her weakness for designer shoes...yet.)

Malcolm noticed the furrow in Catherine's brow. "What I mean is that comprehensive tax planning, in conjunction with financial advice, will provide direction for choosing the right accounts your capital should accumulate in, Catherine," Malcolm's soft voice was reassuring. "If we plan your investment process sagely, not just for today, but with a deliberate longer term strategy, the accountable result – and you'll be very pleased with me when we get there – will be lots of cash flow with manageable taxable income." He wrote the following on the white board:

---

[1] UBS Investor Watch, 3Q 2013

*Retirement planning works best, when it is embraced
by younger people.*

Remember that important principle, he advised. The young have the benefit of time to amass large fortunes in the right tax-exempt or tax-deferred accounts.

Chet was reflecting on the meaning of Malcolm's astute words. "My goal is to be really successful as an investor, and I don't want to second guess myself or my investment choices," he said, after some reflection. "My goal is for us to reach our Wealth Purpose on time and with confidence. I want to know that my money has not been eroded by taxes and inflation and, in fact, has some real purchasing power when we retire or become disabled; heaven forbid. Who knows what drugs and homecare services will cost by then!"

Malcolm agreed. "It's something we all worry about, as provincial governments run deficits and designer prescription drugs that treat devastating illnesses, rise in cost. Those who have true wealth in the future, will invest with the end in mind today: a good understanding of how much they need to save and what it will be worth – after tax and inflation – when they tap into it."

Malcolm returned to the white board to demystify the unique image he drew on it. "Every dollar you make and invest has its own tax home here in this Tax Condo," his eyes twinkled. "Notice, it has four "theme floors" and a tax home for every dollar you're about to make!"

Catherine loved this! "Never thought I'd be thinking about my 'Tax-Efficient Nest' in this way!"

WHAT'S TAXABLE? WHEN?

	TAXABLE	TRANSFERRABLE	TAX EXEMPT
CAPITAL DISPOSITIONS	**TAXABLE** Financial Assets Real Estate Business Assets Personal Use Assets	**TRANSFERRABLE** Financial Assets Real Estate Business Assets Personal Use Assets	**TAX EXEMPT** Principal Residence Qualifying Donated Assets
PASSIVE INVESTMENTS	**REGISTERED** RRSP RESP, RDSP DPSP, RCA, IPP	**NON-REGISTERED** Interest Dividends Rents Royalties	**TAX EXEMPT** TFSA Life Insurance
ACTIVE OR ORDINARY INCOME	**EMPLOYMENT** Salary, Wages, Bonuses Perks and Benefits	**SELF EMPLOYMENT** Net Income Recaptured Depreciation	**PENSION BENEFITS** Superannuation Private Pension Public Pension
SOCIAL BENEFITS	**TAXABLE** Employment Insurance Universal: UCCB**, OAS	**NON-TAXABLE** Refundable Credits	**TAX EXEMPT*** Social Assistance Guaranteed Income Supplement (GIS)

*While Social Assistance and GIS are added to income, they are deducted again before taxable income. Their only affect is to reduce means-tested credits.
**UCCB scheduled to end in 2015.

"Your tax specialist can be of great assistance in guiding your money into the right tax homes, together with your financial advisor, of course; so don't forget to invite me next time you and your father discuss investing within these rooms, Chet. I would love to offer my two cents worth of opinions!"

"More like several thousands of dollar's worth, Malcolm," Chet chuckled, thinking about how much he appreciated this referral to Malcolm from his wise dad, ever the financial planner. "I have read that different income sources we produce – personally or through our investments – will be taxed in different ways. But, just what is the best way to incubate and produce tax efficient income in these various tax homes?"

"Great analogy, Chet; I love the incubation idea. Potential income sources must be housed to align with your Wealth Purpose. The fruit, so to speak, attracts different marginal tax rates, and must be harvested at the right times in your life, to bring you the biggest bounty," Malcolm explained.

He seemed to have worked up an appetite with this analogy. He tossed a red apple over to each of Chet and Catherine and then he polished his against his crisp white shirt.

But, there was Catherine's frown again. "Okay, to better understand this, let's get specific," Malcolm was truly energized both by the apple and by his condo drawing, which was better by far than his last several attempts at visual arts. He turned to it with great pride and invited his captive audience to tour the four floors, explaining the features of each tax home:

Social Benefits. Planning done well, he said, will produce social benefits and tax credits; recall that's a redistribution of your tax dollars to lower income earners – people who meet income-tested ceilings. On the federal level, this can include refundable tax credits like the GST/HST Credit and the Canada Child Benefit (CCB) or the Refundable Child Fitness Credit. Refundable provincial tax credits are available in certain provinces as well.

"The fact that these credits are refundable means you can have absolutely no income to declare at all to receive the money; however, you must file a tax return to receive them," Malcolm reminded the couple. "Remember that non-refundable tax credits are income tested as well; but, in this case, you must be paying taxes to receive any benefit from them." He cited a tax principle to remember:

*Always leverage tax credits
by making new investments with them.*

Active Income Sources: "You will notice that on this floor there are income sources that arise out of your own efforts – your human capital so to speak," Malcolm waved at his drawing. "Human capital diminishes as you get older and your salary or business profits ares replaced with taxable pension benefits. They are accumulated along the way, based on an allowed percentage of your actively earned income. Because they replace that earned income later in retirement, I have put them on the same tax floor. The full amount – 100% – of these ordinary income sources is added to your taxable income. Let's take a closer look. Malcolm was in full instructor mode:

- **Employment Income** – This includes the full amount of wages, salary, bonus, vacation pay, and sick pay. You'll receive a non-refundable tax credit for Canada Pension Plan (CPP) and Employment Insurance (EI) premiums on your tax return, and your employer will be required to remove from the gross income you make, a percentage to pre-pay your tax obligations. These items are shown on your T4 slip when you file your tax return. In fact, the #1 reason why people file their tax returns is to recover over-deducted income tax remittances and overpaid premiums to the CPP and EI.

- **Income from a Business** – It is net business income that you are taxed on – after expenses incurred to earn your top line or gross income. Unincorporated business income is reported on the personal tax return (known as the T1) with your other personal income sources; incorporated businesses file a corporate tax return (known as a T2)

- **Pension Income – Public Sources:** This includes benefits from the Old Age Security (OAS) and the Canada Pension Plan (CPP) which are fully taxable in the year they are received.

- **Pension income – Private sources:** This includes retirement benefits you may receive from an employer-sponsored pension offered at work (also known as a Registered Pension Plan (RPP)). Along the way, your employer will contribute corporate dollars to the plan (that's a good thing!) and you'll contribute too. You may take a deduction for your contributions and you may then also save more from your own efforts. Generally this is done within a Registered Retirement Savings Plan (RRSP), but there is a limit to what you can deduct and save within each plan and when you have both.

Next, he moved to a discussion of passive income from investments. "You have the option to invest your money in three types of homes. We'll get into much more detail in other meetings; but here is what happens to your money at a high level, just so you understand the terms and what each account produces, after tax." He lectured on:

- **Registered Accounts.** Money invested here will feature a tax deferral on investment income. That means, as your principal generates investment income – interest, dividends, or capital gains, for example – there is no tax. Your nest egg grows much quicker as full dollars – unscathed by taxes – are reinvested to earn even more. In the case of the RRSP, you'll get a tax deduction as your investment is put into the account on a "pre-tax" basis. Later, when you withdraw the funds as a pension benefit, both earnings and principal are subject to tax.

With the RESP (Registered Education Savings Plan) and RDSP (Registered Disability Savings Plan) there is no tax deduction when the money is put into these tax homes. However, the government "sweetens the pot" by providing grants and bonds that make your accumulations grow more quickly. Each of these homes comes with special rules, you'll want to understand more fully.

But the best tax shelter of all is the Tax Free Savings Account. There is absolutely no tax on the earnings, ever. When your money is invested, however, there is no tax deduction. That's why it's important to reflect carefully on whether you want to give up a lucrative tax deduction within the RRSP investment to fund your TFSA; or if you want to do both. I'll help you with that decision.

- **Non-Registered Accounts.** Investing in accounts that are not tax sheltered means that you'll need to report the earnings, annually. So for example, when you invest your money in a GIC (Guaranteed Income Certificate) or a CSB (Canada Savings Bond), you will earn interest, which is included in income in full as it accrues. That's right, you will have to add compounding interest to income as it is earned, rather than when it is paid. This makes interest an inefficient investment earning source. It's best earned within a registered plan, in which tax on earnings is deferred, or in a tax exempt account, like the TFSA.

Dividends that are paid to you out of corporate profits left, after tax, are also included in income, but they are subject to special tax treatment to integrate both the personal and corporate tax systems. The dividends are "grossed-up" for income reporting purposes, and then qualify for a "dividend tax credit" to offset the gross-up and reduce personal taxes payable. This integration of the personal and corporate tax systems is not perfect, but allows for a better marginal tax rate on dividends on your personal return.

Other income from property can include net rental income that arises when you invest in real estate. Net rental income is reported – after operating expenses and some allowances for depreciation.

Finally, investing in an insurance policy will usually reap tax exempt benefits to the beneficiaries of the policies. There is no tax deduction for the premiums. But do know that new tax rules will soon shrink the amount of tax exempt income sheltered in universal life insurance policies; earnings above the exempt test will be taxed as passive income similar to earnings from a non-registered account.

Capital Gains or Losses. When you dispose of your assets, either by actual sale or in a deemed disposition (which happens at death, for example, or through an asset transfer) a capital gain over and above the original cost (plus any improvements) may result. Only 50% is added to income however, and only after the capital gains are reduced by capital losses of the current year.

Taxable capital gains can be further reduced when you bring forward unapplied losses of prior years. Reporting losses is therefore important; so is keeping track of them when you have no capital gains in the year. Carrying them forward (or back for up to three years) can be very lucrative. These losses will average down or eliminate the taxes you pay on the disposition of capital assets in your future.

If you are charitable by nature, or have no heirs to pass your assets on to when you die, there are opportunities to avoid reporting capital gains taxation on your gifts, either in kind or as a result of donating the proceeds of sale. It's something we can talk about in more detail at year end, when we are planning your donations.

The Money Moral

When you give every dollar a tax home, and understand how the income it earns is taxed upon withdrawal, you have a selection of options that can be used to average your taxes downward over time, split income with other family members and transfer income as well. This is the proper way to build a Tax Strategy around your Wealth Purpose.

Quickie Tax Quiz

1. How can non-taxable refundable credit be leveraged to arrive at your Wealth Purpose sooner?

2. What role does CPP play in the income streams of an employee?

3. Which type of investment income is most efficient outside of a registered plan or TFSA?

Check out the answers in *Family Tax Essentials Portal* at www.knowledgebureau.com.

MR. & MRS.
EMPLOYED AND SELF-EMPLOYED

It was a really beautiful summer wedding. As Chet and Catherine said their "I do's," their families and friends could not imagine a couple with a brighter future, or more potential to succeed as they took their place in the world together. As they honeymooned in their dream destination of Costa Rica, thanks to all the financial smarts they had already put into place, their proud circle of influence grew into a new village of mutual support.

In their new life as a married couple, Chet and Catherine looked forward to their new careers, and cheering on each other's accomplishments. Chet was moving up in the law firm he was employed at – taking on bigger and more complicated cases, going back to school to specialize in intellectual property law and engaging in community service work where he met interesting stakeholders in his field of passion: international human rights.

Catherine, meanwhile, graduated with honors. She now had a master's of science degree in speech – language pathology and she was excited to begin her work. While the vast majority of graduates in her field would work as employees in hospitals, schools and community centres, Catherine wanted to set up her own private practice and cater to a growing need to help seniors with communications challenges. She would begin with an unincorporated practice, working out of their beautiful new home and she already had a number of relationships set up to focus on her specialty.

As usual, their tax specialist Malcolm featured prominently in Chet and Catherine's future plans; in fact, Catherine was pretty sure she saw tears glisten in his eyes as her dad walked her down the aisle. She was really fond of him – he had become a trusted resource she had much confidence in and so much respect for.

Malcolm had provided two important consulting hours before their honeymoon; one to explain the tax rules around making the most of Chet's employment income and the second to help Catherine set up her home-based consulting business.

He began by explaining the difference between being employed and the self-employed.

"Believe it or not, this is a topic of many tax audits!" Malcolm smiled at his earnest clients. "When you work for someone else as an employee, you are in an "employer-employee relationship." CRA defines this as either a verbal or written agreement to work on a full-time or part-time basis for a period of time, in return for salary or wages," Malcolm said. "What's important is that the employer has the right to decide where, when and how the work will be done by the employee."

In this master-servant relationship, there are several ways to get paid, he continued, noting two key bullets on the white board:

- Taxable income from salary or wages, bonuses or vacation pay, taxable in the year received and

- Tax free or taxable benefits or perks, which can include things like an employer-provided car, employer-provided loans, stock option benefits, paid education, uniforms, meals, memberships to fitness clubs, and so on.

"Employment income is always reported on a calendar year basis; that is, January to December. There are very few exceptions to that rule," he said. "There are two interesting ones, however: employees can defer a portion of their employment income without paying taxes under a salary deferral arrangement in order to take a future sabbatical."

That sounded like an interesting option to Chet and Catherine! "In other cases," he explained, "companies want to reward their best employees. For them, a Deferred Profit Sharing Plan (DPSP) can be set up to share profits of the company. The amounts deposited are not taxable until withdrawn by the employee, after termination or at retirement."

"Aside from that, income from your employer is taxed when received; it's called the 'cash basis' and you'll get a T4 slip reporting your gross income and your source deductions by the end of February. The employer has several obligations to meet in this relationship," Malcolm continued.

He explained that by law, statutory deductions from gross pay must be made for income taxes payable as well as contributions to the Canada Pension Plan (CPP). The employer must match employee contributions. In addition there are withholdings for Employment Insurance (EI). The employer must pay 1.4 times the EI premiums paid by the employee. Usually this happens once a month, although very small businesses have the option to remit each quarter.

"This is obviously expensive for the employer," Malcolm continued, "and so it's not unusual for some firms to want to by-pass those costs and hire independent contractors instead. That's where the tax problems can arise. Over the years, the courts have developed criteria to be used in evaluating whether an individual is an employee or is self-employed." The following questions are a starting point to determine this status, he explained.

- Has the individual entered into a contract of service (an employee) or contract for service (self-employed)?
- What level of control does the payer have over the worker?
- Does the worker provide his or her own tools and equipment?
- Can the worker subcontract the work or hire assistants?
- Is there a degree of financial risk taken by the worker?
- Does the worker have the potential for profit or loss?
- What is the degree of the worker's responsibility for investment and management?
- What does the written contract state?

If an individual can establish that he or she is an independent contractor and not an employee he or she accounts for contracting income as business income, meaning:

- Business-related deductions such as home-office expenses, promotion and entertainment expenses, capital cost allowance on equipment and other such expenses can be claimed.
- Reasonable salaries paid to family members for services rendered are deductible in determining business profits and can be used to split income.

- The owner may incorporate the business and claim the low tax rate applicable to active business income.

- There is no requirement to contribute to Employment Insurance, and there is no ability to draw Employment Insurance during periods of inactivity. Canada Pension Plan contributions are still required.

- Depending on the level of revenue, the business may need to register and collect GST on revenues.

Malcolm shared some recent research. "Did you know that up to 150,000 new business are expected to emerge in the next several years[1] to drive our economy forward? Canada has the lowest insolvency costs in the G20, and is a haven for new immigrant entrepreneurs as well, so we have been a vibrant country to do business in."

Turning now to Catherine, he smiled before he began to speak. She was taking meticulous notes, again. Malcolm's key value proposition in his tax practice was in working with entrepreneurs. He loved their spirit and their vision! That's probably why Catherine enjoyed listening to him so much.

"Business owners are distinct from other types of taxpayers, and I have seen that myself," Malcolm was thinking about the store owners, couriers, beekeepers, chiropractors and so many others he had served in his day. "These are people who invest their time and money first, to reap the rewards of both profit and equity in their enterprises later."

"The Canadian tax system takes this greater degree of risk into account in its tax laws, Catherine," Malcolm was delighted to provide an example. "Business owners can write off business losses against other income of the year; they can also split income by hiring family members to work in their enterprises."

Further, he explained, provided the business is structured as a qualifying Canadian Controlled Private Corporation (CCPC), each shareholder may also qualify for a lucrative Capital Gains Exemption of over $800,000. "Make that a million if you are a qualifying farmer or fisherman!" Malcolm exclaimed. "That's a terrific reward for the risk the business owner has taken in investing in the business."

---

[1] Ernst & Young G20 Entrepreneurship Barometer 2013.

"When is income from the business considered to be received for tax reporting purposes?" asked Catherine. Malcolm thought this was a particularly good question. It gave him the opportunity to talk about some areas of tax law that can bring on tax disputes and court challenges.

"For most very small businesses taxable income will be reported when revenues are received in the calendar year. This is called the 'cash basis' of reporting income," he explained. "But, the money doesn't have to be physically received. It can come through an agent, be deposited directly in your bank account and so on. It is basically considered to be taxable to you when it has physically left the payor's hands. That's an important principle when we deal with money in transit in cyberspace."

"The accrual method of reporting income, on the other hand, is used by most businesses and for reporting income from compounding investments." Under the accrual method, he told them, income is reported when earned (whether or not received) and expenses are deducted when incurred (whether or not paid). "That would apply to you, Catherine, if you still want to be self-employed, that is."

Catherine nodded. She had just put up her last office pictures and set up voice mail on her new office phone. She was ready for her first client consultation proposal, which she would get right down to in the morning.

Even though it was barely mid-September, Malcolm wanted Catherine to download a tax form from the CRA website: Form T2125 *Statement of Business or Professional Activities*. This form did a pretty good job of itemizing the kinds of income and expense entries she would need to make at tax time and Malcolm wanted Catherine to start saving receipts and records properly.

He wanted to remind her to treat her business like an individual: start its own banking records and credit card payments. Malcolm also wisely counselled Catherine to determine whether her services would be subject to GST/HST. He then provided her with a checklist of discussion points for their next meeting:

Business Start Discussion Points

1. When did the business start?

2. What is the fiscal year end?

3. Is there a formal business start plan?

4. Are you keeping meticulous records of income and operating expenses?

5. Are you tracking interest on business loans or lines of credit?

6. Have you kept a separate record of purchases of assets and operational expenses?

7. Are you keeping track of "in-kind" transactions?

8. Are you keeping a daily business journal?

These opportunities to document networking activities, marketing and sales initiatives, the interviewing of staff and suppliers and the auto distance travel logs that chronicled business travel, all would be required to prepare an audit-proof portfolio.

The Money Moral

Know the difference between employed and self-employed taxpayers. The self-employed enter into contracts for service with their clients. This person works independently and is not subordinate to anyone who oversees the nature of the work or the results. That's quite different from the employer-employee relationship in which the employee enters into a contract of service.

Quickie Tax Quiz

1. What is the difference between an employed person and a self-employed person in CRA's eyes?

2. How much does the employer have to contribute to CPP on behalf of an employee? EI?

3. What is the difference between "cash basis" and "accrual method" reporting of income?

   Check out the answers in *Family Tax Essentials Portal* at www.knowledgebureau.com.

FROM ORDINARY INCOME
TO CAPITAL

Chet hadn't visited with his father, Thomas, for a while, but this evening was a special one: Chet had received a promotion at work and he and his father were enjoying an early dinner to celebrate.

"Most people begin their financial career just like you have, Chet, by earning money through an employment contract. By investing in yourself, and your ongoing education and career advancement, you'll just keep earning more. That's a marker of sound career advancement; a goal most people have as they progress at work, and it's a good one."

Thomas paused to collect his thoughts and articulate clearly. "But, if you can remember these general principles, you can turn your ordinary employment income, which is 100% taxable, into assets which allow you to grow your Wealth Purpose more quickly." Thomas explained:

1. With few exceptions, when you create income, you create taxes.

2. As income rises, taxes increase.

3. When you use income to create capital, the value of the assets accumulates without taxation, until they are disposed of.

4. Certain income sources produced from those assets, are taxed more favorably than ordinary employment income.

Chet nodded, fascinated. He wondered how he could more quickly build his asset base, when his key source of income was from employment.

"If you can find a way to build on your investment in your employer's company, by participating in stock options, for example, or the company pension plan and/or the perks and benefits available to you, you'll soon start building both income and equity."

That was thought-provoking. Chet was most interested in the perks of employment he might be able to negotiate for with his employer next time his contract came up for renewal.

"As you know," he father continued, "corporate income is taxed at much lower rates than personal income and so anytime an employer can pay for any of your costs of consumption – from lunches out with your clients to group health benefits and an employer-provided vehicle, you benefit from corporate tax efficiency – your employer's lower corporate dollars have been used to provide remuneration to you."

Chet was particularly interested in an opportunity to negotiate for a company car, and perhaps some tax-free birthday gifts! The premiums to his company's private health care plan were already in place, and were very valuable to his new family unit, as Catherine did not have coverage in her self-employment. Chet also wanted to get more education, so he was interested in discussing the tax-free opportunity here, as well. He understood that, provided the courses benefited his employer, he could receive a tax-free tuition benefit.

Chet thought he'd discuss this with Malcolm the next time they got together, later this week, before he signed his new employment contract. When he got there, Malcolm put another easy-to-understand chart in front of Chet, itemizing benefits he thought might be of interest in his employment negotiations:

Perks of Employment

Taxable Benefits*	Tax-Free Benefits
Personal use of employer's vehicle	Recreational facilities, including social or athletic club memberships
Gifts in cash or those that exceed $500	Non-cash gifts under $500; $500 more for birthdays, anniversaries. Annual $1,000 total.
Value of holidays, prizes and awards	Employee counselling services for health, retirement or re-employment
Premiums for a provincial health or hospital plan	Premiums for a private health plan or lump sum wage loss replacement plan
Tuition paid for courses for personal benefits	Tuition paid for courses for the employer's benefit
Interest-free and low-interest loans	Certain moving expenses if required by the employer
Group sickness, accident or life plans	Employer's required contribution to provincial health and medical plans
Gains and income under employee stock option plans	Employer-paid costs of attendant for disabled employees or to cover away-from-home education due to work in remote worksites

* If these amounts include GST/HST, employees who are allowed to claim employment expenses may be able to claim a rebate on Line 457 by filing form GST370. If you receive this rebate, report it as income in the following tax year on Line 104.

"Let's take a look through the taxable benefits, first," said Malcolm, "as you are particularly interested in a new car. You'll be taxed on those benefits, known as a 'standby charge', but this charge can be reduced if personal driving averages less than 1,667 kilometres per month. Reimbursements for supplementary business insurance, parking or ferry/toll charges are all received tax free."

This was certainly worth noting. Chet was also very interested in exploring whether an interest-free or low-interest loan from his employer might be available to help with his investment activities. He understood that the difference between a market rate of interest and the employer-provided loan would be a taxable benefit. But, if the loan is used for investment purposes, including an investment in an employer's stock, for example, a deduction for the amount shown as a benefit on the T4 slip can be claimed as a deductible carrying charge.

"Remember, the value of a deduction rises with your income," Malcolm reminded his client. "If your marginal tax rate is 40%, reducing your income with a deduction for carrying charges provides a 40% tax saving... it's like getting 40 cents of each interest dollar paid back."

Chet of course already knew about his statutory source deductions, those required under law: Canada Pension Plan (CPP) and premiums for Employment Insurance (EI). He would have the opportunity to claim a non-refundable tax credit for his portion of the premiums when he files his tax return. But the real value of those non-refundable credits was capped at the lowest tax rate federally and provincially.

But employers can make other deductions from gross pay. This can include contributions to employer-sponsored Registered Pension Plans (RPPs), or contributions to Registered Retirement Savings Plans (RRSPs). This was another way to build wealth by taking advantage of the employer's low-taxed dollars.

In each case, a tax deduction would result for Chet while income earned in both plans would be tax deferred. Any RPP contributions would show up on the T4 Slip; RRSP contributions would be confirmed with an official received from the financial institution. Chet understood that he would have to plan his RRSP contributions carefully, to take into account any contributions made to the RPP. But that was a subject for another meeting.

In the meantime, Malcolm added a list of CRA form names to encourage Chet to learn more about his potential deductions from employment income. They seemed to fly right out of the top of his head with melodic ease:

"We'll use Form T777 to claim Employment Expenses, Form T1-M in case you ever move more than 40 kilometres to a new work location and Form TL2 if you get sick of lawyering and decide to become a long distance truck driver." They both chuckled.

The discussion next turned to the employee who works from home. Chet often had the opportunity to do so. "With so many more employees working out of their home offices, there are big lessons in tax savings are in those legitimate claims for home workspace expenses and auto expenses," Malcolm offered. "But employees must account for both personal use and business use of the related expenditures meticulously, in much the same way self-employed people manage their affairs. Of course, that means recordkeeping!"

Chet was pretty good at the auto log dilemma. "I would use my car's navigation system and Google Maps to figure out the distance between my workplace and my business appointments. But how would I account for trips that originate from my home office?"

Malcolm explained that driving to and from his home to his employer's workplace was considered "personal" in nature. However, if the appointment to see the client was between home office and workplace, a business distance segment was legitimately claimed.

"One more thing: to claim any out-of-pocket expenses in pursuit of employment activities requires your employer to complete Form T2200 *Declaration of Conditions of Employment*," said Malcolm as the two men rose to end their meeting and shake hands. "Let me know if you'd like me to negotiate your perks and benefits for you with your employer."

Chet hadn't thought of taking his tax advisor along to negotiate his employment contract, which on reflection, seemed to be a novel idea. There was something else bothering him though. He had been thinking about that average $1,700 refund they discussed last time they were together; a chunk of money which wasn't going into his pocket, but rather, straight into CRA's every week before he got paid himself.

"Isn't there anything we can do to reduce our tax withholdings so we get to use more of our money right away? It really is hard to save money on your own when the government takes such a big chunk. I honestly would forego my refund if I could just invest that money every two weeks into my RRSP."

It was a good question, a great insight and Malcolm had a great answer. "Indeed!" Once again he pulled up two forms from his computer: The TD1 *Personal Tax Credits Return* and the T1213 *Request to Reduce Tax Deductions at Source*.

"Your payroll department should make sure you update your TD1 *Personal Tax Credits Return* every year, generally in December. This will provide instruction on how much tax is to be withheld from your pay – monthly, bi-weekly, semi-monthly, etc. – depending on the payment frequency chosen by your employer."

"It's semi-monthly in our firm's case," Chet responded.

Malcolm went on to explain how important it is to be proactive about notifying the employer when things change: a new spouse, or a new dependant all can create changes to the TD1 form, which result in tax withholding reductions. The benefit? More take-home pay during the year, instead of waiting for a refund next year when they file their taxes, means more money to invest all year long.

Employees can also request to have less tax deducted at source by their employers for deductions that are not listed on TD1. In order for the employer to withhold reduced taxes, the employee must complete the T1213 form, *Request to Reduce Tax Deductions at Source*, and submit this to the Taxpayer Services Division of their tax service office, along with all supporting documents.

If the Canadian Revenue Agency (CRA) is in agreement, they will send a letter of authorization to the employee, and this should be given to the employer, who can now reduce tax withholdings. A new T1213 must be submitted to CRA each year. However, where the deduction being claimed relates to deductible alimony or support, the CRA may issue an authorization to cover two taxation years.

Chet took the forms along as he finally took his leave; calling Catherine to apologize for his late arrival for dinner.

The Money Moral

Any time you can negotiate for tax free or even taxable benefits, you'll avoid paying for the consumable goods and services you receive with high taxed personal dollars, and that's a good thing! So is making sure you pay only the correct amount of withholding taxes.

Quickie Tax Quiz

1. In order to claim employment expenses, your employer must certify that you are required to pay those expenses. What form is used for this?

2. Under what circumstances can the standby charge taxable benefit for use of an employer-provided car be reduced?

3. What happens if you work for more than one employer and subsequently contribute too much to CPP or pay too much in EI premiums?

Check out the answers in *Family Tax Essentials Portal* at www.knowledgebureau.com.

STRETCH EMPLOYMENT INCOME
WITH TAX
DEDUCTIONS

Chet and Malcolm's next visit was over coffee, watching the first snowflakes of the year. The topic was tax deductible out-of-pocket expenses. Chet was required to spend money negotiating contracts on behalf of his employer, and those activities often took him out of the office and in various meeting places with clients.

Together they examined the T777 *Statement of Employment Expenses* form which Malcolm pulled gingerly out of his now wet bag.

"Employees are subject to numerous restrictions in claiming any expenses against income; always under the premise that it is the employer who is responsible for controlling the work the employee does and providing the workplace and necessary tools," he explained.

In general, employees may not claim asset acquisition costs. There are three exceptions to this rule: the purchase of vehicles, musical instruments or aircraft used in performing the duties of employment. "I'll let you know when I'm thinking of purchasing my first jet, then," Chet wise-cracked.

"My point is this, sir," Malcolm smiled to make this point: "It is wise tax planning to lease computers, cell phones or other equipment if used to earn employment income. You won't get a tax benefit on your return, otherwise."

Chet made the note in on his iPad. He also learned that when an employee is required to pay for out-of-pocket expenses, the Form T2200 *Declaration of Conditions of Employment* must be signed by the employer before a write-off is possible.

Malcolm later emailed some tax filing facts to help Chet with his recordkeeping, as employee on salary only had different rules – much more restricted – in claiming out-of-pocket expenses, than employed commission salespeople and self-employed people:

What Expenses Can Employees Claim?

A. Employees on Salary Only

- ☐ **accounting fees,** but not including income tax preparation
- ☐ **legal fees** may be claimed if incurred to establish a right to collect salary, wages or a retiring allowance or pension benefits, but these costs may not exceed the amount of those sources that you report in income. Any non-deductible components may then be carried forward and deducted in any of the seven subsequent tax years in which further income from these sources is reported. When pensions or retiring allowances are transferred to an RRSP, the deductible legal expenses are limited to the amount not transferred.
- ☐ **motor vehicle expenses** (including Capital Cost Allowance (CCA) – the tax equivalent of depreciation, interest or leasing costs, as well as operating costs), but only if the employee is not in receipt of a non-taxable allowance for the use of the motor vehicle
- ☐ **travel expenses,** including rail, air, bus or other travel costs, meals, tips and hotel costs, providing the excursion is for at least 12 hours and away from the taxpayer's metropolitan area. Meals and tips are subject to a 50% restriction.
- ☐ **parking costs** (but generally not at the place of employment)
- ☐ **supplies** used up directly in the work (stationery, maps, etc.)
- ☐ **salaries paid to an assistant** (including spouses or children if a salary equivalent to fair market value is paid for work actually performed)
- ☐ **office rent or certain home office expenses.**
- ☐ **tools** acquired by employed mechanics are generally not deductible, however a special rule exists for new tool costs incurred by apprentice vehicle mechanics and tools acquired by tradespersons.

B. Salary Plus Commission or Commission Only

□ **All of the above** plus

□ **income tax preparation costs,**

□ **legal fees** incurred to defend charges incurred in the normal course of business, and

□ **auto and travel expenses,** are allowed only if these employees are required to pay their own expenses and regularly perform their duties away from their employer's place of business. However, the expenses are categorized into two groups: deductible travel and deductible sales expenses. This is because you cannot claim sales expenses that exceed commissions earned in the year.

Deductible travel expenses allowed include:

- **Auto operating expenses** like gas, oil, repairs and fixed costs like licenses, insurance, interest, leasing and capital cost allowance. The latter three expenses are limited to annual maximums if a passenger vehicle is used. See Auto Expenses in the next section.

- **Travelling expenses** such as the cost of air, bus, rail, taxi or other transportation, which takes the employee outside the employer's metropolitan area. However, travel expenses are claimable only if the employee does not receive a tax-free travel allowance.

If you're only claiming auto expenses and travelling expenses, the total of the two amounts may exceed commissions earned and excess expenses may be used to offset other income of the year.

Deductible sales expenses allowed include the expenses above plus:

- promotional expenses
- entertainment expenses subject to a 50% restriction for the personal component of the expense
- home office expenses

When you have a claim for sales expenses under this category, claims may not exceed commissions earned in the calendar year except for interest and capital cost allowance on a motor vehicle.

The Money Moral

Employees may claim certain unreimbursed expenses of employment but Form T2200, *Declaration of Conditions of Employment*, signed by the employer, is required for each year in which tax-deductible expenses are claimed. This form must be kept on file for CRA to review. In addition, employees are subjected to a restricted list of possible expenses; in particular asset acquisitions.

Quickie Tax Quiz

1. Can employees write off tax preparation fees on their tax returns?

2. Which expenses, if claimed by a commissioned salesperson will limit their claim to the amount of their commissions?

3. What special rule applies to the claiming of meals and tips?

   Check out the answers in *Family Tax Essentials Portal* at www.knowledgebureau.com.

CLAIMING
AUTO EXPENSES

One of the milestones Catherine and Chet were very excited about this year was a new car for Chet. They had discussed this with Chet's boss. As part of his compensation in his new position, the company would lease the car and Chet would be assessed a "standby charge" for his personal use of the automobile.

Catherine, meanwhile, was quite excited about taking possession of Chet's SUV for use in her business. She had researched its fair market value when the new car came up for Chet and found his car was still worth a handsome $35,000.

Catherine and Chet were hesitant about disturbing their affable tax specialist, but Chet wanted to understand the tax cost of this wonderful perk being offered to him. Malcolm was reached via speaker phone from his holidays in Florida.

"No need to apologize, happy to help as always," he said.

Malcolm explained that a "stand-by charge" would have to be calculated. Had the car been purchased by Chet's employer, the math would have been 2 per cent of the cost of the vehicle per month, for as long as Chet has access to the vehicle. "That makes it pretty expensive to drive a beater," Chet laughed.

"You're quick, Chet, that's for sure!" Malcolm chuckled. "But, because your vehicle will be leased, the standby charge is calculated at two thirds of the monthly lease cost and it will be that number which is added to your taxable income. You should know, however, that if your personal use of the auto is minimal, we will apply for a reduced standby charge. To qualify, your annual personal driving must not exceed 20,000 kilometres. We will also need to show that you are using the car primarily – that is, more than 50% – for business purposes."

Malcolm then provided an example. "If you drive the car 25,000 kilometres a year for business purposes, for example, and 15,000 kilometres a year for commuting to and from work or going to the lake, for example, the standby charge can be reduced. I will use Form RC18E to make the calculations for you."

"In addition, if your employer pays for some of the operating costs, like your gas, oil, maintenance or insurance, a taxable benefit may be added to your income if you do not reimburse for these costs within 45 days after the end of the tax year. The benefit is determined as a flat per-kilometre rate, regardless of how or how much the employer paid for the expenses," Malcolm explained. "The reimbursement back to your employer may make sense if he pays only a small portion of the expenses. We will do the math on that too, when I get back."

The conversation then turned to the actual mechanics of the tax return Chet and Catherine would have to file to account for the auto news. The process was going to be similar for both Chet and Catherine as they used their two vehicles in pursuit of income. "We're both obviously going to be keeping a distance log – that's not negotiable, right honey?" Chet smiled at his documentation-challenged young spouse.

"Automotive expenses can only be deducted if they are not reimbursed by the employer; also, no additional claim is allowed to an employee who receives a reasonable allowance for the use of the vehicle. That's why we need to do some calculating for you, Chet, when I get back." Malcolm said. "Otherwise, a deduction is allowed on the tax return for employees who pay their own auto expenses and are required to use their vehicle in carrying out their duties of employment."

Malcolm explained that this is verified to CRA on Form T2200 *Declaration of Conditions of Employment*. Here the employer will state that the employee must use the auto for employment purposes and is responsible for paying auto expenses, does not receive a reasonable allowance for auto expenses, and will not be reimbursed for them (if there is a partial reimbursement, this must be accounted for).

"Most people will have used their vehicle for both personal and business/employment purposes. It is necessary to keep that meticulous auto log which records distance driven for both purposes, for at least one year (the base year). After this," Malcolm explained, "you can keep the records for as few as three consecutive months, Catherine." One could visualize Malcolm's mirthful wink.

"So long as your driving patterns do not vary on either side by more than 10% in a subsequent year, you will be able to claim the ratio determined by the formula," he said as he scrawled and explained:

$$\frac{\text{Current year ratio for log period}}{\text{Base year ratio for same period}} \times \text{Base Year full-year ratio}$$

Personal use includes vehicle use by other family members, friends, etc. In other words, total personal use of the vehicle is assessed, not just the use by the person using the auto for business or employment.

"When there is a 'mixed use' of the car, the expenses are first totalled. This is based on your actual receipts and a log of cash expenditures, like car washes for example. Then the total costs are pro-rated by the allowable business use ratio." Again a formula followed:

Total Allowable Expenses x Allowable Business Use Ratio

"What can I claim for my auto expenses?" Both Chet and Catherine wanted to know, but Catherine asked first. She dreamed of an expensive foreign sports car and all the write offs that would bring. Unfortunately, Malcolm burst her bubble a bit!

He explained that, as a self-employed person, she would add the fair market value of Chet's car to a special schedule upon which a depreciation amount would be calculated. Malcolm called it the "declining balance" method of claiming Capital Cost Allowance (CCA), another interesting tax term, they would discuss every year.

"There are two types of auto expenses that can be claimed: fixed and operating, and this can have an important effect on the type of car you buy or lease and how much money you spend, Catherine," Malcolm warned. He scanned over an Auto Expense Fact sheet after their call, which Catherine and Chet studied carefully:

Tax Fact Sheet: Claiming Automobile Expenses

A. Fixed Expenses include:
☐ Capital Cost Allowance (subject to a maximum cost of $30,000, plus taxes)
☐ leasing costs (subject to a maximum of $800 a month, plus taxes)
☐ interest costs (subject to a maximum of $300 a month)

B. Operating expenses include:
☐ gas and oil, tires, maintenance and repairs
☐ car washes (keep track of coin operated washes)
☐ insurance, license fees
☐ auto club memberships
☐ parking (generally parking expenses incurred for business purposes are fully deductible and not subject to a proration for personal component)

Malcolm had put a note into the corner of his scan: "'Cents per kilometre' claims are not allowed for but can only be used in specific instances where a 'simplified method' is allowed. These include claims for medical travel or certain moving expenses."

He also pointed out for Catherine: "How much you can claim for fixed expenses is restricted, as you can see, so your deductible claims will depend on the cost of the car you drive and for what purposes you use it. Because of this, the first rule to remember when buying a car 'for tax purposes' is that you may not be able to write off the full cost if it is a luxury vehicle. Sorry, Catherine."

The Money Moral

Claiming auto expenses for employment or self-employment purposes can be tricky, but will embellish cash flow, if done astutely. Always enlist the help of a tax professional the first time you make the claim and before year end, to get the best after-tax results.

Quickie Tax Quiz

1. For how long must an auto log be kept?

2. What fixed auto costs are restricted?

3. What is the difference between an operating expense and a fixed expense?

   Check out the answers in *Family Tax Essentials Portal* at www.knowledgebureau.com.

CLAIMING
HOME OFFICE EXPENSES

A home office is a reality in both employed and self-employed careers these days. People are driven to work 24/7 for a variety of reasons: technology allows it; we operate in a global economy; it's tough to get everything done during the workday.

Nonetheless, there are very specific rules for claiming home workspace expenses, as Catherine and Chet were soon to find out. Malcolm used his white board to draw sample spaces in the home which could be legitimately claimed and to explain eligibility criteria:

"Chet, to qualify to make home workspace expense claims for an employee, the space must meet one of these two basic criteria:

- The workspace must be the place where the individual principally (more than 50% of the time) performs the office or employment duties, or

- The workspace must be used exclusively in the period to earn income from the office or employment and, on a regular and continuous basis, for meeting customers or other persons in the ordinary course of performing the office or employment duties."

"Catherine, for a self-employed person to claim home workspace expenses, the space must meet one of these two criteria:

- the workspace must be the principal place of business, which means 50% of the time or more,

- the workspace must be used only to earn business income and must be used regularly and on an ongoing basis to meet with customers."

"You will note the criteria are virtually identical." He then drew a sample office space on the white board, resembling roughly, the verbal description Catherine was giving him. "To determine the amount of deductible home office expenses, total expenses for the costs of maintaining the home are pro-rated. Here's the fraction we use to do that, Catherine:"

$$\frac{\text{Sq ft of the home workspace}}{\text{Sq ft of the entire living space}} \times \text{Total Eligible Expenses} = \frac{\text{Deductible}}{\text{Expenses}}$$

"Chet you should know that the rules differ slightly for you, because you are employed. Should you decide to claim a home workspace, consider the following:"

Employees who do not earn commission may claim:
- utilities;
- maintenance and repairs, including light bulbs and cleaning supplies; and
- rent.

Commissioned sales employees can claim:
- utilities;
- maintenance and repairs, including light bulbs and cleaning supplies;
- rent;
- insurance; and
- property taxes.

Self-employed people can claim:
- utilities;
- maintenance and repairs, including light bulbs and cleaning supplies;
- rent;
- insurance;
- property taxes;
- interest; and
- capital cost allowance

Malcolm provided a warning at this time, however. "Please take special note that making a CCA claim on your principal residence will compromise the principal residence exemption, so it's usually not a good idea to claim this and so we won't."

"Oh yes, there is one more thing!" Malcolm loved telling a little tax trivia sprinkled within his broad tax strokes. "An employee may not claim home office expenses that exceed income from the employer. That shouldn't be a problem for you, Chet."

Then he faced Catherine. "But for you, young lady, a special rule: a self-employed person may not create or increase a business loss with a claim of home office expenses. But the good news is that non-deductible home office expenses may be carried forward (indefinitely) to reduce income from that employer (or business) in subsequent years."

As usual, Malcolm concluded with a smile, and his usual parting advice: "Don't forget to save all the receipts – okay?" and Catherine and Chet left his office knowing a lot more about keeping and saving their money.

The Money Moral

If you work out of your home office, set aside a separate area used exclusively for those purposes for a potential home workspace claim on your tax return. Then claim operating expenses according to your taxfiler profile.

Quickie Tax Quiz

1. If Chet worked evenings and the odd weekend in his den, can he claim home office expenses?

2. If Catherine operates her business out of a rented office in a strip mall and also regularly meets with clients evenings in her home, can she claim home office expenses?

3. Which of the three groups identified here may not claim mortgage interest as part of their home office expenses?

   Check out the answers in *Family Tax Essentials Portal* at www.knowledgebureau.com.

TAX SAVVY
ENTERTAINING

As Chet and Catherine settled into their careers, there were long hours and many interesting cases to look after. The newlyweds cherished their time together on the weekends; it often felt like they were two ships that passed in the night; exhausted but happy. They were each entertaining more often now, building their networks meeting clients and other professionals after work.

"I've been meticulous about logging the distance I'm driving for work-related activities, have you, Catherine?" Over a rare couple's dinner out one weeknight, Chet playfully tapped Catherine's toes under the table, knowing that his young bride had trouble with the word "meticulous" as it related to recordkeeping of any kind. "What about your entertaining expenses, are you remembering to keep the credit card chits?"

Catherine recovered from her cringe and smiled sweetly. "Well yes, I take a picture of every one of them with my phone, darling husband," Then she feigned mock outrage at the very suggestion that her process was suspect.

"Actually I have been meaning to ask Malcolm a couple of questions about these expenses; perhaps you know the answer? I understand that claiming the costs of entertaining clients is legitimate, but how far can I go... for example, can I write off the cost of those exquisite shoes I bought for the charity function we are going to later this month? After all, they are certain to attract attention with potential new clients!"

Chet bit his tongue; he really didn't want to know how much the shoes had cost, and he was not entirely sure how to answer his wife's question. "Well, Malcolm will help us soon with our year-end tax planning; let's ask him... although I am quite sure the shoes are a personal and non-deductible expense, dearest wife!"

On their next visit, Chet and Catherine brought Malcolm a giant Christmas wreath, featuring a large red bow with the name of Catherine's business artfully scripted in gold lettering on it. They knew how much Malcolm loved the season. Thanksgiving had come and gone and Malcolm was chomping at the bit to put office decorations up already, something his office assistants were able to successful wave off so far. "Bah Humbug" certainly was not in Malcolm's vocabulary!

They settled in for a rare cup of hot chocolate, to herald in the first real frost of the season, and to provide a little bit of therapy to Malcolm. He needed to confess his sins about the Christmas cookies his wife thought she was hiding in the family freezer. "She thinks I can't smell them," Malcolm winked, "but, I am really hoping one day I can tell her they taste pretty good frozen, too!" Malcolm put a hush finger up to his lips as Chet and Catherine giggled at his sneaky savvy.

"Thank you very much indeed," Malcolm exclaimed as he admired the beautiful wreath and gingerly laid it on the coffee table. "I hope you saved the receipt for this lovely piece, Catherine. It's a beautiful promotional piece for your practice and I will display it prominently for all my clients to see – I hope your referral business rises exponentially!" His voice seemed to rise and boom in mirthful pre-season exuberance. "I will look for the receipt when we do your taxes early next year. This gift to your merry old accountant will surely be tax deductible."

The next tax lesson, about to begin, was all about deducting entertainment expenses. "Self-employed taxpayers and employed commissioned salespersons may deduct reasonable amounts for consuming food and drink associated with their business activities, including taxes and tips," Malcolm began, peering over those glasses in his charming way, "and yes the cost of restaurant gift certificates for employees or clients are included here. But there is a catch... "

Chet and Catherine humored Malcolm with mock shock as their breaths shortened in anticipation of his next line: "Your deduction for these costs, Catherine, is limited to 50% of the amount you actually paid."

"Really?!" Catherine couldn't hide her actual surprise. She had a terrible poker face. Her new husband chuckled as he drew that to her attention, while whispering in her ear. "Yes, for example, if you take your client out for a $100 lunch, you would claim the whole amount on your return, but our tax software would restrict the amount to only 50% on the tax form."

"I see," said Catherine. Malcolm went on. "Remember, though, that CRA's auditors may deem that $100 lunch to be unreasonably expensive, in which case, they have the arbitrary right to limit your deduction to 50% of the amount CRA determines to be reasonable."

"No kidding!" Catherine and Chet exclaimed together. "Absolutely true," said Malcolm. He suggested that it's not a bad idea to keep a log showing that personal lunches are much cheaper by comparison, justifying the business lunch scenario as reasonable.

Malcolm also went on in some detail to inform Chet and Catherine about other costs incurred by business in entertaining prospects or clients; deductible when conducting business but also subject to the 50% limitation:

- tickets for a theatre, concert, fashion show; athletic event or other performances
- the cost of private boxes at sports facilities; or hospitality suites
- the cost of room rentals to provide entertainment, such as a hospitality suite;
- the cost of entertaining business guests at night clubs, athletic, social and sporting clubs and on vacation or business trips;
- the taxes, gratuities, and cover charges related to these entertainment costs.

"Are there any exceptions to the 50% rule?" Chet was wise to tax complexity – there were the rules, and then there were the exceptions, it seemed!

"Yes indeed," came the response, as Malcolm finished his hot chocolate and rose to address the white board in his office. "Take note, my young protégés!" he smirked.

1. **Consultant's Billings.** Malcolm explained that if a consultant pays for food and beverages while working away from the normal place of business, bills those costs to the client for re-imbursement, the costs are then included in the consultant's income, and 100% of the costs of the food and beverages may be deducted.

2. **Meals at Conferences.** Malcolm was sure these two would be attending many conferences in their careers. He told them that when an all-inclusive fee is paid for food, beverages and/or entertainment, a deductible $50 amount is allocated for each day of the conference, and this amount is subject to the 50% restriction. All other costs of attending the conference are fully deductible, but there is another limit: only two conferences can be deducted per year.

Malcolm embellished. "For example, let's pretend you paid $3,500 to attend a five-day business conference that was all-inclusive, Catherine: meals, entertainment, and lodging were included in the conference fee. What is the maximum amount of meal and entertainment expenses you are permitted to claim?"

"Well," said Catherine, "The answer is simple: as no amount was specified separately for meals and entertainment, I would claim only $250, and then your software would make sure that of this amount only 50% was claimed. So by my calculations my maximum deduction for this conference is $3,375 (= $3,500 – ($250 x 50%))."

"Brilliant!" Malcolm exclaimed, almost in unison with Chet. "Now here's another dark horse for you to remember: there is no 50% limitation on the cost of meals and beverages served, or entertainment provided on planes, trains or buses."

"What about ships, boats, or ferries?" Malcolm shook his head at Chet. "No, the 50% rule will apply here." Chet really didn't understand how he could keep all these little details in his head, and had great admiration for Malcolm's terrific memory. There were a few more exceptions to the 50% rule Malcolm wanted to impart to his clients:

- **Medical and Moving Expenses.** When you are making legitimate claims under these provisions, there is no 50% restriction in claiming travelling expenses.

- **Employer-Sponsored Events.** Employers who provide food or entertainment for staff members, as well as their spouses and children, may deduct 100% of these costs, but in this case the event must be available to all staff members. There is also another restriction: the employer can have no more than six of these events per year; after the sixth the 50% rule kicks in again.

- **Employer-Operated Restaurants or Cafeteria.** If you operate a restaurant or cafeteria, however, the costs of food and beverages provided to your employees will not be restricted to the 50% rule, again only so long as the food is made available to all employees. Any subsidized meals, will however represent a taxable benefit to the employees, which we will account for on their T4 slips.

"That's where you come in, Chet," Malcolm swung around dramatically to face his client. "Well, it's about time you noticed I was here too... seems like you've spent the meeting speaking only to my lovely wife!" This time Chet winked.

"That's because employees can't claim meals and entertainment in the same way as self-employed people," came the retort. "I challenge you to look up section 8 of the *Income Tax Act* and find out more, although here's a bit of a summary for you," Chet knew Malcolm was just hamming it up for them now.

"The 50% limitation will be used by employees in claiming deductions against employment income in four specific instances, only one of which you might qualify for Chet, and that's the last one:

- paragraph 8 (1)(e)-These are away-from-home meal expenses of railway employees;
- paragraph 8 (1)(f)-These are expenses of commission salespersons;
- paragraph 8 (1)(g)-These are the away-from-home meal expenses of certain transport employees; and
- paragraph 8 (1)(h)-These are travelling expenses of employees who are ordinarily required to work away from the employer's place of business in conducting their affairs."

"In each of these cases, form T2200 *Declaration of Conditions of Employment* is required, signed by the employer. But it's worthwhile to take a moment now to really understand how employees claim travelling expenses including the cost of meals and entertainment, Chet." Malcolm seemed to be asking for permission to go on.

"By all means, continue, Malcolm."

"Travelling expenses for your purposes will include food, beverage, and lodging expenses but not motor vehicle expenses. They are treated separately on the tax forms," said Malcolm. "You will only be able to deduct travelling expenses if you meet all of the following conditions, something that most employees find shocking, when their entertainment expenses are disallowed by a tax auditor. I can think of several high rolling stockbrokers in this category, who are employed by their financial institutions and so are subject to these same limitations." A list of criteria was discussed:

- You must first of all be normally required to work away from your employer's place of business.

- Your employer will not have paid you a non-taxable allowance for travelling expenses. The tax department describes a non-taxable amount as one that is reasonable under the circumstances.

- Under your contract of employment, you will have agreed to pay your own travelling expenses, and you will need to keep with your records a copy of Form T2200, *Declaration of Conditions of Employment*, which has been completed and signed by your employer.

"One more important thing; you'll find this hard to believe and so I'll read it to you from CRA's website: 'You can only deduct food and beverage expenses if your employer requires you to be away for at least 12 consecutive hours from the municipality and the metropolitan area (if there is one) of your employer's location where you normally report for work.'"

Malcolm went on to explain one of the perils of his work: so many employees think they can write off all their unreimbursed travelling expenses, including meals and entertainment, and he has lost of few clients who their relatives or friends who would prepare their returns with the full claims.

"Unfortunately, I usually see these folks again, when they ask me to help them with the tax audit. Class dismissed!" Malcolm shooed Catherine and Chet out of the office as he realized he was late for his next meeting.

"One more thing," Malcolm's hand turned into a stop sign. "No matter how fancy the shoes, unless you are a professional dancer, Catherine, there's no deduction for the expense, sorry." How did he know? Catherine turned to her husband who was now dashing out ahead of her. "Hope you got them on sale, dear!" The first voluminous snowflakes of the season had started to fall in the meantime and Catherine delighted in the accuracy of her snowball...

The Money Moral

Despite the fact that tax lore is rampant, it's important to understand the fine print when it comes to claiming meals, entertainment and conference expenses. The 50% rule is usually caught by tax preparation software, but it's in the exceptions – the claiming of the 100% amounts – that errors can occur. Professional tax advice, especially at year end, can help to solidify audit-proofing efforts.

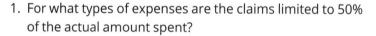

Quickie Tax Quiz

1. For what types of expenses are the claims limited to 50% of the actual amount spent?

2. What are the criteria for an employee to claim travel expenses?

3. What limitations are placed on the claiming of all-inclusive conference fees?

Check out the answers in *Family Tax Essentials Portal* at www.knowledgebureau.com.

WHEN RELOCATING
CLAIM MOVING EXPENSES

Moving to a new residence is one of the most stressful events a new couple will encounter. In fact, for many people, moving ranks right up there with some of life's most stressful events, such as the death of a loved one, and divorce or separation.

Catherine and Chet were about to find that out, but through the eyes of Catherine's parents. They were downsizing and relocating to Tofino, where Catherine's father would continue to work and her mother would retire to her gardens and charities. They had closed on a new condo overlooking the ocean – a very spectacular view just outside the city.

It was a dream come true, but major upheaval and lots of decisions stood before them: purging, packing, travelling and ultimately, painting and decorating. Catherine was sure the latter would be a real test of their longstanding partnership. Her father loved order and peace; his artistic wife relished the chaos that came with making their new house a home.

Catherine's mother was challenged with recordkeeping, too. "At least you can see I came by it honestly," Catherine would say to her shrugging husband. Catherine's parents didn't have time to see Malcolm before the move, but Catherine brought it up when they met Malcolm at a community charity event.

"There is a silver lining in all of this upheaval, because moving expenses can be tax deductible in some instances," Malcolm said after asking Catherine how her parents were doing. "Being able to recoup some of your money at tax filing time, does help to take some of the sting out of the move. In fact, leading edge tax advisors can help families keep track of moving costs in this chaotic time by scanning receipts into electronic drawers courtesy of their tax software," he offered with a kind smile. He pledged to send along a thorough email to help Catherine's parents. It began with his usual dry humor:

"According to your offspring, the move is going well, but your tax documentation is at risk. Catherine thought you might like to know what's deductible as you move. For you, Victoria, the answer is nothing, so you don't have to worry about a thing!" Chet and Catherine could feel the merriment in his virtual smirk as he addressed Catherine's mother first, and her relief at being released from the pressure of keeping receipts.

Of course, there would be more; Malcolm really couldn't help himself. "But for your husband, who will have income at your new location, there is good news, which will save you a lot of tax dollars and therefore will assist with the decorating costs... but you must keep all the receipts for costs." Malcolm began to explain the rules, with his usual thorough overview:

"The moving expenses deduction is very lucrative and it is available to employees, self-employed people and students, as long as their new home is at least 40 kilometres closer to the new work location than the old home was. As long as income is earned at the new location, in the form of salary, wages, self-employment income or taxable student awards, you can make this claim on your tax return."

"That also means that if you earn only investment income or employment insurance benefits at the new location, you will not qualify for the deduction. Here are some little known eligible moving expenses. Try to remember some of them – tax trivia can make you really popular at Christmas parties and impress your new neighbors!"

Chet and Catherine looked at one another and smiled. They concurred with one another that this certainly this could be true for Malcolm; but neither of them could fathom Catherine's parents actually pulling something like this off. The email boomed a headline next:

Deductible Moving Expenses

1. The costs of selling your former residence in the old location: this includes really big expense items like real estate commissions,

the penalties for paying off a mortgage, legal fees and advertising costs.

2. The costs of keeping a vacant old residence that you haven't been able to sell (but only to a maximum of $5,000). This includes costs you continue to incur while you are actively trying to sell: mortgage interest, property taxes, insurance premiums, heat and power, for example.

3. The expenses associated with purchasing the new home (as long as the old home was owned, rather than rented, that is), including transfer taxes and legal fees.

4. Temporary living expenses (including meals and lodging – not subject to the 50% rule) for up to 15 days while you are waiting to move into your new home.

5. Transportation, removal and storage costs including insurance for your household effects

6. The costs of meals en route (again 100%, no 50% restriction)

Another, bolder headline followed:

What's Not Deductible:

- Costs incurred to make your former property more saleable – like repairs or staging your home
- Losses on the sale of your former property
- Expenses incurred before the move (such as house hunting or job hunting)

Malcolm concluded with some additional investing advice for Victoria.

"Should you find that you wish to go back to school once you get settled, we should speak about the *Lifelong Learning Plan* within your RRSP, as a way to fund those studies on a tax free basis. You should also know that students moving to attend full-time courses at a post-secondary school may claim moving expenses against the taxable portion of research grants or other awards (such as prizes for academic achievement) or any income earned at summer jobs or your employment or self-employment while going to school."

Finally, some advice for the young couple: "Chet, if your employer ever decides to move you to another city, we should chat about negotiating for the firm to pay for your moving expenses. Sometimes a claim for out-of-pocket moving expenses is also possible in that case, but this would be reduced by the amount of any company re-imbursement. So planning for receipt-keeping is definitely in order, if a move is in the cards for you."

The Money Moral

Discuss the opportunity for tax relief from moving expenses with your tax advisor before the stressful ordeal be-gins so you can be sure to keep all those receipts next year, when tax filing time arises. Moving expenses are very likely to be audited if you claim them, so be sure to mark the tax receipts box prominently.

Quickie Tax Quiz

1. How far must you move in order to make a claim for your moving expenses?

2. What is the maximum claim for moving expenses?

3. If your closing on your old home is on the 4th of the month but your possession date for your new home is on the 20th, how much of the costs incurred between those dates can be claimed?

   Check out the answers in *Family Tax Essentials Portal* at www.knowledgebureau.com.

MAKE HAY WHEN THE SUN SHINES:
MAXIMIZE RETIREMENT PLANNING

People with wealth maximize every opportunity to build capital accumulations throughout their lifetime. One excellent way to do so is by participating in an employer-sponsored pension plan. This can also be known as a Registered Pension Plan (RPP). Chet was lucky to have one at his workplace.

"Not only does your employer contribute pre-taxed dollars into the plan with you, the earnings in the plan accumulate on a tax-deferred basis," Patricia, the human resources manager at his firm was stellar at explaining the nature of the plan and patient with Chet's curiosity about it. "The result of this is that your wealth grows exponentially over time, leveraging your efforts here with the corporate dollars invested for you. Having an RPP, though, can impact your ability to save separately in a private Registered Retirement Savings Plan (RRSP) through what is known as a Pension Adjustment or PA. Be sure to look for that on your T4 Slip and your Notice of Assessment from the CRA."

Chet was beginning to understand that company pension plans come with a host of new terms. Patricia and Malcolm together were terrific resources for a proliferation of tax strategies that emanated from the RPP, RRSP, and TFSA savings opportunities:

"First, know right at the starting gate, that the TFSA is not impacted by your contributions to an RPP or and RRSP," Malcolm informed Chet. "It always pays to maximize your opportunities in the TFSA and it will, in fact, make you a millionaire retiree if you do." Catherine's ears perked up at the word "millionaire".

"Here's what you're looking at if you save faithfully in the TFSA. I've used a contribution of $5500, invested every January 2. Make this the first good thing you do for your future every year right after the other New Year's resolutions you are sure to break!" It was spooky how well Malcolm seemed to know his clients. "Here's a chart to illustrate what I mean:"

TFSA Investment*: $5500 a Year for 40 Years; 10% Average Return

Taxable Income	Total Balance in TFSA	Taxes Saved by Investing in TFSA	Comparison: Balance in Taxable Account	Additional Returns in TFSA
$58,000	$2,677,685	$1,538,323	$1,139,362	57%
$90,000	$2,677,685	$1,851,859	$825,826	69%
$140,000	$2,677,685	$1,913,241	$764,444	71%

*rounded; Ontario residency

It was clear the TFSA made sense as a cornerstone of any retirement income plan. Chet and Catherine resolved to save here for their multi-million dollar retirement.

"Let's discuss now how to maximize your employer-sponsored pension, Chet." Malcolm started to explain over coffee and leftover Christmas sweets. "When you contribute to your employer-sponsored RPP, there will be deductions withheld and remitted into the plan for your portion of the contributions; and yes, you guessed it, this comes right off the top of your gross pay. But that's a good thing: whole dollars from your efforts and your employer's pre-tax profits are going to work for your future."

He explained that he would deduct certain amounts based on Chet's current year services to his employer, and that this would be shown in Box 20 on the T4 slip. His tax software would post this amount to Line 207 of the tax return to claim a deduction. His T4 slip would also show his Pension Adjustment in Box 52 which would be used by CRA in determining his RRSP/PRPP contribution room for the following year.

"I will explain what the PA is in a moment, but here is an important tax planning concept: The deduction you receive for this RPP contribution, and any additional RRSP contribution you are allowed to make will increase your tax refund. You can use that extra cash flow to top up your TFSA contribution." This sounded like a great plan to Chet and Catherine.

"Sometimes companies allow you to make past service contributions, too. You should check into this, Chet. Those contributions are also deductible in the year and will be included in Box 20." Malcom next explained a complicated set of rules, challenging Catherine not to glaze over entirely. Chet's elbow in her side ensured she stayed focused.

"Your claim for such contributions is limited as follows: you cannot claim more than *$3,500* less any other contributions deducted in the current year (current and past service while not a contributor). But any amount contributed that cannot be deducted in the current year may be **carried forward** and claimed in a future year according to these same rules." Malcolm wrote the bolded words on the board. "It's important to keep track of that, something our tax software is very good at."

He further explained that any interest paid to make those past service contributions in instalments is deductible for tax purposes as if it were part of the past service contributions, forming part of the complicated limitations for deductions he had outlined above for past service contributions.

"Let's turn now to managing an RRSP contribution when there is an RPP." Chet felt Catherine's pulse to make sure she was still with them. She smiled, assuring him she was okay with all of this.

"It's important to understand that you may not be able to contribute to your own RRSP, depending on how much was contributed to your RPP, Chet, so let's be sure you don't over-contribute in error. That can create the need for some fuss including withdrawals and some complicated forms. You'll need to understand what the PA, PSPA and PAR acronyms are if you want to understand how the RPP and the RRSP provisions interact, so you can maximize contributions to each. Or you can simply ask me to tell you exactly what you should contribute to maximize your tax savings as part of our year end planning."

Malcolm proceeded to explain the terms:

- **What's the PA?** When you contribute to a Registered Pension Plan or your employer contributes to your plan, your RRSP contribution room for the following year is reduced. The amount of the reduction is called a Pension Adjustment (PA). The amount of your pension adjustment is shown in Box 52 or your T4 slip. This will not affect your current-year RRSP contribution limit as it is based on your income in the prior tax year, but it will reduce your RRSP contribution room earned this year and available next year.

- **What's a PSPA?** If you make past service RPP contributions, those contributions will also reduce your RRSP contribution room earned in the following year. The reduction is called a Past Service Pension Adjustment (PSPA). You'll receive a T215 slip showing the amount. This will affect your RRSP contribution room for the following year and will be reflected in your RRSP contribution limit as indicated on your Notice of Assessment. Most software does not include the T215 form as it does not affect the current year.

- **What's a PAR?** In some cases, when you cease to be a member of a RPP and the benefits you receive from the plan are less than your accumulated pension adjustments, you'll receive a Pension Adjustment Reversal (PAR). The PAR is reported on a T10 slip and increases your RRSP contribution room for the current year.

Key Benefits to an RRSP Contribution. Malcolm stopped here to turn from his next new headline on the white board to face his young clients again. "There are many benefits to making contributions to RRSPs, not the least of which is getting a larger tax refund so you can put away the most money possible to work for your own future. Consider these pluses:" He turned back to his work on the board, highlighting several bullets, and then embellishing verbally on each:

- **The Tax Deduction.** RRSP/PRPP contributions result in an immediate tax deduction for the principal, which reduces your tax bill in the current year, as well as your net income on Line 236. This means you'll potentially receive more in refundable and non-refundable tax credits.

- **The Tax Deferral on Earnings.** RRSP/PRPP deposits accumulate and grow on a tax-deferred basis (that is, earnings within the plan are not taxable until they are removed from the plan).

- **Caution:** Taxes Payable on Withdrawal. If possible, withdrawals of RRSP principal and earnings should happen in a year when your marginal tax rate is lower than the year of contribution to get the best tax results.

- **More Than a Retirement Plan.** Money may be borrowed on a tax-free basis from your RRSP to fund the purchase of a new home under the *Home Buyers' Plan* or to finance post-secondary education under the *Lifelong Learning Plan*. Many people don't know this; but this can be good investment, as long as you are prepared to return the money into the RRSP on the required payment schedule or sooner. Remember, there's no tax-deferred accumulation if the funds are not in the plan.

- **Income Splitting Opportunities.** Starting at age 65, RRSP pensions may be split with your spouse to reduce the taxes that will become payable. If you use a spousal RRSP along the way, making sure that RRSP accumulations are equal, you'll get better tax results down the road. In this case, the higher earner takes the RRSP deduction based on his or her larger contribution room, which can provide tax planning opportunities during child rearing years or later when one spouse become age-ineligible for making RRSP contributions. That happens at the end of the year in which you turn 71. There are special withdrawal rules, however, when a spousal RRSP is used in planning. The annuitant must wait three years from the last spousal contribution to withdraw the funds, or the money is taxed back to the contributor. There is an exception to this rule: when the spousal funds are transferred to a Registered Retirement Income Fund (RRIF) or an annuity to start providing retirement income.

Earned Income for RRSP Purposes. Malcolm was ready for the next part of the lesson, which would explain the restrictions the government has put into place for maximum RRSP contributions.

"The primary restriction, is that you must have 'earned income' in the prior tax year to contribute to an RRSP this year," Malcolm embellished: "If you earn income from employment, self-employment, net rental income, CPP disability income or taxable support payments last year, you will have 'earned income' for RRSP/PRPP purposes this year." He then turned to the white board to emphasis the rather complicated rules under a new headline. "Remember: each year that you have earned income, you create RRSP/PRPP contribution room which you can use the following year."

Maximum RRSP Contributions. The contribution room generated is the lesser of:

- **18% of your earned income** for the prior year to an indexed annual dollar maximum (for example, $25,370 for 2016; contributions based on 2015 income), less

- **any pension adjustments (PA)** from your employer-sponsored plans in the prior year. This is shown on Box 52 of the T4 slip.

"What if I don't have any income in the year, perhaps because the expenses in my business were too high," asked Catherine. "Do I have to use my RRSP contribution room and take a deduction? Perhaps I can carry it back and offset last year's income?"

"All good questions, Catherine," Malcolm relished in explaining the rules. "RRSP contribution room is cumulative, so if you generate contribution room by virtue of your earnings, but don't use it by making your maximum RRSP/PRPP contribution this year, the full amount of your unused contribution room gets carried forward and you can make a larger contribution in a future year. That provides you with interesting cash flow planning opportunities. However, RRSP contribution room and deductions cannot be carried back. The CRA won't allow 'retroactive tax planning' with an RRSP."

It turned out, much to Catherine and Chet's relief, that CRA makes the tracking of the available RRSP contribution room easy, especially if you have an employer-sponsored RPP. They also understood the rules for making the contributions, which Malcolm reiterated on the white board:

Contribute to your RRSP throughout the year, or within 60 days of the year end to claim a tax deduction.

"Each year your Notice of Assessment or Reassessment from CRA will show the maximum contribution that you can make for the next taxation year. This will include the 'unused' room from the past, 18% of your earned income to the current dollar maximum, and adjustments due to changes in your RPP contributions or employer contributions to your PRPP," Malcolm said as he concluded his lesson on becoming a millionaire with savings in the TFSA, RPP and RRSP. "Our tax software will also keep track of this for you in your carry forward screens, so we'll discuss the numbers each year together when we meet for year-end planning."

Then he explained the rules to follow in the rare instance of an over-contribution to the RRSP: "Taxpayers age 18 and over may over-contribute up to $2,000 over their normal RRSP contribution room without penalty. That's a good idea, as more of the income in the plan can be sheltered from taxes. But if your RRSP over-contribution exceeds $2,000 at any time, you are considered to have made an 'excess contribution' which is subject to a penalty tax of 1% per month. I like to avoid this like the plague, as the form that is required to calculate the payment of the penalty is a nightmare!"

A final piece of sage advice ended this visit on a high note. Malcolm found room on the white board for a final headline: Reducing Your Source Deductions, and an important moral:

> *Remember, you're only required to pay*
> *the correct amount of tax, no more.*

"Recall that when you contribute to your RRSP, you can reduce your withholding taxes at source so you essentially get your tax refund with every paycheque," he looked directly at Chet. "Let's make arrangements for that in your financial plan; then I will complete Form T1213 *Request for Reduction in Tax Deductions at Source* for you. This will put more money in your pocket every pay period, to assist with your savings plans."

Malcolm closed with this: "Becoming wealthy over your lifetime to secure your financial future, has as much to do with maximizing your take-home pay as it does with negotiating employment benefits your employer can pay for you with low-taxed corporate dollars. Maximizing those opportunities to leverage the equity in your employer's firm is an important way to Make More and Own More."

The Money Moral

Retirement planning is for the young. When you put your money in the right "retirement bucket", you will have pre-planned your tax efficient retirement income. Making sure you maximize your savings in a TFSA, RPP and RRSP will propel forward your peace of mind in retirement, which means, your Life Purpose and your Wealth purpose can intersect sooner.

Quickie Tax Quiz

1. What types of income increase your RRSP contribution room?

2. How do contributions to a Registered Pension Plan affect your RRSP contribution room?

3. What happens to your RRSP contribution room if you don't make any contribution for the current year?

   Check out the answers in *Family Tax Essentials Portal* at www.knowledgebureau.com.

SPEND AND SAVE,
BEFORE TAX

You have learned through the eyes of Chet and Catherine that it is "ordinary income" that is taxed at the highest level: the full amount (100%) of your gross income from employment is added to the tax return's total income. In addition, the full amount of the gross pension benefits that replace your employment income once you are retired are added to income.

The employment and, later, the pension income you get to keep is eroded by taxation, right at source and off the top, before you get to spend any of that money. That's why digging for every deduction and tax credit you are entitled at tax filing time to is so important. These efforts directly increase your cash flow, which is the money you have in your possession to spend and save with.

Average taxpayers pay a heavy price for their after-tax dollars. In the absence of a sound Tax Strategy, the choices they have to live their preferred lifestyle are limited. They are people who are forced to live paycheque to paycheque not just through their early earning years, but in retirement too. This is completely avoidable, if you choose to do both, spend and save, before tax.

When you make it a priority to save more employment dollars in an RRSP or an employer-sponsored RPP (Registered Pension Plan), for example, you will generate a bigger tax refund you can use for the choices that improve your lifestyle today, or better yet, tomorrow. Investing that refund into a Tax Free Savings Account, for example, can make you a millionaire over time.

When both you and your spouse maximize your TFSA,
you could be multi-millionaires in your lifetimes.

But sometimes things go wrong in the choices people make with those tax salvaged dollars. They are willing to pay non-deductible interest on credit card purchases, after already paying taxes on the money. That makes spending very expensive.

Here's an example to illustrate: Assume you make $100 after taxes, representing at an effective[1] tax rate of 30%. You would have had to make $143 before taxes, to have those 100 dollars in your hands today. If you now went out to buy a $100 pair of shoes, and then charged them to your credit card, they cost you $143 in real human capital – before adding the sales taxes. But that is only true if you paid off your credit card at the end of the month. Let's say you are in the habit of paying off only your minimum balances, and your credit card company charges you a 30% interest rate on the outstanding balance. Your shoes have actually cost you $186 or more plus sales taxes.

Now take a moment to calculate your hourly rate paid at your employment. If it's $45 an hour, you'd have to work more than four hours for those shoes. If it's $15 an hour, you'd work almost 17 hours for that one pair of shoes... you'd really have to think long and hard about whether they are worth it.

An important side note: bankers tend to lend money to people who have high net worth statements; less to people who can show no wealth accumulations at all. In fact, credit is very expensive for those people, especially if credit card debt is the only type of borrowing they have, and none of it is tax deductible.

Catherine and Chet learned early in their relationship with Malcolm, their tax advisor, that certain sources of money are completely tax exempt. That included any redistribution of social benefits – tax credits they qualified for when filing their returns – or amounts received from gifts and inheritances, life insurance benefits received on the death of a loved one and gains on the sale of their principal residence.

In addition, any of the income earned within a TFSA – Tax Free Savings Account – is completely tax exempt, as the name implies.

---

[1] That means, that in the example, progressivity has been taken into account: the fact that income is subject to a tax free zone or Basic Personal Amount on the first dollars and then a progressively higher rate of tax is paid as your income rises past various tax brackets)

That certainly makes a good argument for using funds saved within a TFSA to fund non-deductible purchases, like larger personal-use items. Because you don't lose your TFSA contribution room when you remove funds from the plan, you can pay off credit cards, avoiding expensive interest charges, and then save back into the plan. The only caveat is that if you don't have available contribution room, repayments may have to wait until the following year when the withdrawal amount is reinstated as contribution room.

Cash flow that comes from tax exempt income has
a higher value to consumers.

On the other hand, leaving your money in the TFSA to earn compounding investment income that is never taxed, will guarantee for you, a million-dollar-plus retirement – completely tax free – all depending on how soon you invest and the length of time the money is accumulated in the plan. Your rate of return on the investments in the plan is important too. Fine tax planning in conjunction with sound financial planning will bring you to your Wealth Purpose much sooner in life.

Having a Tax Strategy provides the BIG difference between being
exceptional and being average in building your financial future.

Taxpayers and their advisors will next want to discuss the various taxable earned income levels required to maximize tax preferences and credits and in that way, expand their cash flow. The Essential Family Tax Facts provide recent income ceilings that are meaningful in those discussions. Most important in considering the choices you have to spend and save in investment accounts other than the TFSA, understand the following:

Income is Taxed Now; Wealth is Often Taxed Later.

While employment and pension income is taxed heartily and immediately, your accrued values in assets are not taxed at all; until you sell or otherwise dispose of your assets, that is. So, it follows, that what's important in reaching your Wealth Purpose, is to focus as much on building wealth as you do on building income.

So why generate high taxed employment income at all, you might wonder? Many wealthy people don't. Their income may in fact be low on the tax return itself, but behind this lie large asset values accruing on a tax free or tax deferred basis. For those folks, inflation is a big eroder – it functions much like a tax, and over time can put a real dent into asset values, because taxes are paid on these inflated values. That's why investors are always looking for returns that beat both taxes and inflation to achieve purchasing power in the future.

But there are important reasons to generate just enough taxable income, but no more. In deciding how much income to create for tax purposes and from which sources, remember that actively earned income from employment or self-employment is required to fund certain other income sources or remuneration, as well as to claim certain tax deductions and credits, all of which are of benefit to you in your future. Consider the chart below:

Income Benefits Created by Earned Income	Tax Deductions, Credits and Benefits Related to Earned Income
• Canada Pension Plan (CPP) benefits	• Deductions for RPP, RRSP, union or professional dues, child care expenses, moving expenses, employment expenses
• Employment Insurance benefits	• Disability Supports Deduction
• Certain perks of employment including Employer-sponsored retirement pensions, also known as Registered Pension Plans (RPP).	• Working Income Tax Benefit
• Registered Retirement Savings Plan (RRSP)* for yourself and your spouse	• Refundable Medical Expense Supplement
• Deferred Profit Sharing Plan (DPSP) income	• Canada Employment Amount
• Individual Pension Plan (IPP) income	• Pension Income Amount
	• GST Credit

If you have the opportunity to invest employment dollars in accounts that earn a variety of investment income sources, you have the potential to earn income that is taxed at lower marginal rates than employment or pension income. Taken all together, you will have the opportunity to *average down* the taxes you pay on all your income sources together; and that increases dollars to spend with.

Your investment choices also include the building of equity in a business you own or are a part owner of. Taxes are paid on net profits of the business, not the gross revenues earned. Net profit (or loss) is arrived at after deducting reasonable expenses incurred to earn business income.

There is no finite list of business deductions. The *Income Tax Act* allows business owners to deduct *any reasonable expense* that is incurred to earn business income. This includes, in general, the salary and benefits business owners pay their employees. Salaries paid to spouses and children, if in line with what non-arm's length employees are paid under the same circumstances for work needed and actually performed, also qualify. So you can pay your family members to work in your business, deduct their salary or wages to reduce the income from the business, and pay taxes on the net profits left. That's a great way to share the full value of the first dollars you have earned.

For these reasons, any time if your employer offers to pay your costs of consumption for business purposes along the way or remunerate you with perks that enhance the qualify of your life – be that social or athletic club memberships or group health benefits – you should be sure to participate. This is true of your opportunity to leverage your employer's generosity in providing pension savings as well.

Those first dollars earned in a business can also be used to buy or lease company cars, reimburse travel, hotels, education, entertainment – a host of legitimate expenses that are related to the earning of gross revenues. But personal expenses are not deductible to the business owner and in the case of employees will be added to income as a taxable benefit. In the case of "mixed use" expenditures, like auto or home workspace expenses, an allocation for any personal use must be made before business expenses can be claimed.

The Money Moral

Tax-astute employees will make sure current and future needs are adequately met through their employment, earning just enough taxable employment/pension income to maximize tax preferences and benefits, and then focusing on opportunities to build equity by investing in income-producing assets that can provide tax exempt, tax preferred or tax deferred returns.

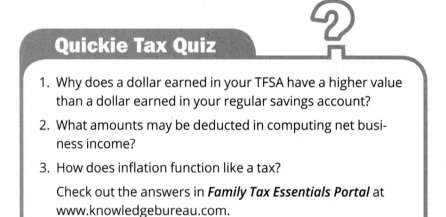

Quickie Tax Quiz

1. Why does a dollar earned in your TFSA have a higher value than a dollar earned in your regular savings account?

2. What amounts may be deducted in computing net business income?

3. How does inflation function like a tax?

   Check out the answers in *Family Tax Essentials Portal* at www.knowledgebureau.com.

THE MONEY MORALS:
GIVE EVERY DOLLAR A DECENT JOB

Control the First Dollar You Earn, Then Invest It. A big tax refund is a bad thing, especially if you could be using the money to grow for you in an appropriate tax home all year long, rather than waiting until several months after the calendar year end for repayment of the interest-free loan you gave to the government. Be sure you pay only the correct amount of tax, no more, all year long.

Know How Your Income is Taxed, and When. When you give every dollar a tax home, and understand how the income it earns is taxed upon withdrawal, you have a selection of options that can be used to average your taxes downward over time, split income with other family members and transfer income as well. This is the proper way to build a Tax Strategy around your Wealth Purpose.

Know the Difference Between Employed and Self-Employed Income. The self-employed person enters into contracts for service with their clients. This person works independently and is not subordinate to anyone who oversees the nature of the work or the results. That's quite different from the employer-employee relationship in which the employee enters into a contract of service.

Use Low Taxed Dollars to Build Wealth. Any time you can negotiate for tax free or even taxable benefits, you'll avoid paying for the consumable goods and services you receive with high taxed personal dollars, and that's a good thing! So is making sure you pay only the correct amount of withholding taxes.

Employers Must Verify Out-of-Pocket Expenses. Employees may claim certain unreimbursed expenses of employment but Form T2200, *Declaration of Conditions of Employment*, signed by the employer, is required for each year in which tax-deductible expenses are claimed. This form must be kept on file for CRA to review. In addition, employees are subjected to a restricted list of possible expenses; in particular asset acquisitions.

Claim Auto Expenses, but with a Log. Claiming auto expenses for employment or self-employment purposes can be tricky, but will embellish cash flow, if reported astutely. Always enlist the help of a tax professional the first time you make the claim and before year end, to get the best after-tax results.

Home Office Claims are Common. If you work out of your home office, set aside a separate area used exclusively for those purposes for a potential home workspace claim on your tax return. Then, claim operating expenses according to your tax filer profile: employed, employed commission salesperson or self-employed person.

Entertainment Expenses Come with Restrictions. Despite the fact that tax lore is rampant, it's important to understand the fine print when it comes to claiming meals, entertainment and conference expenses. The 50% rule is usually caught by tax preparation software, but it's in the exceptions – the claiming of the 100% amounts – that errors can occur. Professional tax advice, especially at year end, can help to solidify audit-proofing efforts.

Moving Expenses Can Be Lucrative. Discuss the opportunity for tax relief from moving expenses with your tax advisor before the stressful ordeal begins so you can be sure to keep all those receipts next year, when tax filing time arises. Moving expenses are very likely to be audited if you claim them, so be sure to mark the tax receipts box prominently.

Save in Registered Accounts, Funded by Employers. While you are never too old to start saving and planning for your retirement, retirement planning is optimized when you are young. When you put your money in the right "retirement bucket", you will have pre-planned your tax efficient retirement income. Making sure you maximize your savings in a TFSA, RPP and RRSP will propel forward your peace of mind in retirement, which means, your Life Purpose and your Wealth purpose can intersect sooner.

Focus on Increasing Both Income and Capital. Tax-astute employees will make sure current and future needs are adequately met through their employment, earning just enough taxable employment/pension income to maximize tax preferences and benefits, and then focusing on opportunities to build equity by investing in income-producing assets that can provide tax exempt, tax preferred or tax deferred returns.

PROCESS CHART: How to Give Every Dollar a Decent Job

Here is an allocation chart for you to think about how to best use each dollar you earn, along with a benchmark percentage. What job are you giving each of your hard-earned dollars? Will one spouse's income do to provide the funding for both your Life Purpose and your Wealth Purpose?

Putting Every Dollar to Work	Benchmark %	Your %
Taxes	25%	
Non-Discretionary – Food Clothing Shelter	30%	
Discretionary – Registered Retirement Accounts	18%	
Capital Pool – Other Investments	10%	
Transition Pool – Risk Management – Insurance	2%	
Wealth Purpose – Fun, Philanthropy	15%	

PART 4 – SAVE

LEVERAGING
GOVERNMENT
GIFTS

It was Chet and Catherine's first Sunday dinner as a new blended family. Catherine's parents, Juri and Victoria, had been invited, and Catherine was soundly embarrassed. The creamed cauliflower her mother-in-law so lovingly made for her, as it was her favorite thing, was making her feel very sick indeed. She was trying hard to stay in the conversation around the table.

It began with a toast and congratulations all round for Catherine's athletic father, Juri, who was enjoying his new semi-retirement on the "Wet Coast." He was going on about how much he wished that he and Victoria would have had the good fortune to invest in a TFSA when they were younger.

"If you and Catherine contribute to your TFSA regularly and to the annual maximum throughout your lifetime, you will have a completely tax free pension when you retire, Chet – putting you light years ahead of our generation of savers," he correctly observed.

Malcolm, the family's trusted tax accountant agreed. He had been invited to dinner, as well. Juri and Victoria were so pleased to meet him, after his wonderful email advice during their move to the coast. Amazingly, he always seemed to be able to do the math for any financial discussion in his head. Tonight, the lovely wine with dinner seemed to spur on the prowess as he spoke about the virtues of the TFSA.

"This opportunity to invest in a TFSA has only been around in Canada since 2009. Every young adult resident of Canada may reserve for themselves the opportunity to become a multi-millionaire in his or her lifetime. Being very conservative, by depositing only $5,000 each year (and indexing this amount by 2% with inflation), for 50 years at a 4.5% interest rate, the balance remaining for you after the last deposit, will be over $1.2 million dollars. But if you invested just a little bit more every year, say $5,500, and at a higher average rate of return, you would be a multi-millionaire within your lifetime."

Malcolm went on to recite an example he had shown a new 25-year-old client he met with just in the past week. The young man was already a successful investment advisor with a brokerage firm. He wanted to plan a quick route to his Wealth Purpose, which was to definitely retire at age 65. He was anticipating a 10% return on his TFSA investments held over this 40 year period.

"The math was incredible," Malcolm boomed. "We could see that he would accumulate approximately $2.7 million in that time period, assuming an average 10% rate of return. More eye-popping were the extent of the tax savings at his average income level of $90,000. If the money was saved in a taxable account instead of the TFSA, about *70% less money* would be available for his future: approximately $1.8 million in taxes were saved by accumulating in the TFSA account. We hadn't even adjusted for inflation yet, but the numbers were very sound. My client would get to multi-millionaire status 10 years sooner, too. "

This was clearly incredulous. Chet dreamed about buying a second residence for the family somewhere warm with a golf course nearby... at the age of 55 instead of 65. The TFSA was a non-negotiable financial play for him.

The conversation quickly turned to the flexibility within the investment itself. "Despite the fact that you might think this is too good to be true, investors may take the money out of their TFSA for whatever purpose they wish and then put the money back into the TFSA to grow some more. Unlike your RRSP, you do not lose your TFSA contribution room when the money comes out," Thomas chimed in.

Not to burst his bubble, Chet gently chided his dad: "Yes, but aren't there penalties for 're-contributing' at the wrong time?" Indeed, this was true. Malcolm explained that you do have to wait until the required contribution room is created again: January 1 of the next year.

Before the family could protest, Chet's dad, Thomas, launched into his rather strong opinion on why he thought every investor should choose a TFSA as a perfect investment for their future dreams.

"It's really frustrating that more people don't take advantage of this opportunity to build millions in savings in their lifetime. Did you know that the TFSA has gained broad-based acceptance by 40% or 11 million average Canadians who invest in it? I read through the last federal budget and learned that more than 80% of all TFSA holders have incomes of less than $80,000." He put down his fork and folded up his napkin, all to make a dramatic point: "What this means, however, is that 60% of Canadians are missing out on this golden opportunity to become truly wealthy. What a shame!"

Thomas went on to explain that there were so many opportunities to build not just individual wealth, but also, family wealth using the TFSA. "You see, this account is also exempt from the normal 'Attribution Rules.' Chet, you may recall that this is a special rule that requires higher earners to report income from the investment of any capital that is transferred or loaned to their lower earning spouses or minor children."

At this point, Catherine rose to excuse herself from the table. She was looking a pale shade of green. "Everything okay, dear?" Victoria's voice rose gently with concern. "No, but I soon will be mom, don't worry," came Catherine's hasty reply.

In her absence, Thomas wanted to provide his top tax reasons why no one should miss populating their TFSA contribution room every year. Chet's mother, Beverley, a soft-spoken lawyer by profession, and Catherine's mother Victoria made a rare exit, to check on Catherine in the meantime. The white board in Thomas' home office was once again prolifically decorated with Tax Strategy:

Reason 1 – Family Income Splitting: "As we discussed at the dinner table, there is no attribution rule attached to the TFSA because all resulting income is tax exempt. So this is a great opportunity to transfer capital to each adult child in the family; something I often mention to my clients who are wealthy parents or grandparents."

Reason 2 – New Tax-Sheltering Opportunities Retirees: Malcolm jumped in with another tip. "Tax sheltering of income earned within an RRSP cannot continue after the year in which you turn 71. Investors then have to convert their RRSP to a RRIF (Registered

Retirement Income Fund) or an annuity and start drawing a periodic and taxable benefit. What this means is that even if they don't need the money, they are forced to take these taxable withdrawals into income. It's a good idea, though to move that money into a TFSA after the tax reporting, to grow the earnings again – and faster – in the TFSA."

Reason 3 – Avoid High-Income Tax Brackets and Surtaxes: Chet was interested in this tip as it was clear his earnings were rising at the firm and that the governments – both federal and provincial – seemed to think that introducing high income tax brackets and rates was the newest trend!

"Savings within a TFSA are also a great way to reduce ongoing income tax burdens by sheltering investment earnings when you are young," his father said. "but the TFSA is also an important wealth preservation tool for seniors and their heirs. During life, up to 50% of untaxed RRSP or RRIF accumulations can be split with a spouse but not until the recipient is 65. At death of the first spouse, the accumulations role over to the surviving spouse on a tax-free basis. But when that second spouse dies, all remaining tax-sheltered accumulations must first be added to taxable income before distribution to the remaining heirs."

Chet learned that this "deemed disposition" at death can bump the income of the final return into the top tax brackets. "Much better to 'average in' taxes payable from registered accounts along the way and then reinvest the money that's left, after tax, in a TFSA," said Malcolm, as Thomas nodded in agreement. "This will often limit high tax obligations for the heirs of the surviving spouse."

Reason 4 – Estate Planning Considerations: TFSA vs CPP. Thomas moved on to compare the Canada Pension Plan to the TFSA at this point. "You know, son, when you continue to work past age 60 you have to contribute to the Canada Pension Plan even if you are taking taxable retirement benefits out of the plan. You have the option to continue to fund the CPP between the ages of 65 and 70 if you are working, just like Juri may be thinking of doing. But this is not a great plan if both Juri and Victoria have contributed the maximum to their CPP account over their lifetime. Should something happen to one of them, there will be no additional survivor benefit paid from all the contributions you have made."

This was astounding to all the men in the room, especially Juri. "You mean, my pension benefits are completely lost to Victoria – she will get no additional survivor benefit if I die – because she also qualifies for the top CPP retirement benefit?"

"Afraid so," said Malcolm. "However, while investments in the TFSA lose their tax-exempt status and become taxable after the death of the plan holder, a rollover opportunity is possible when the spouse or common-law partner becomes the successor account holder. This rollover will not be affected by the spouse's TFSA contribution room, and will not reduce the surviving spouse's existing TFSA room either. That makes funding a TFSA instead of the CPP a better move, if you have the option."

The men were refilling their wine glasses to continue the discussion when suddenly all three women reappeared. Catherine had re-gained the pink glow normally perched on her cheek-bones and Chet rushed to her side with a big hug. He noticed the tears in Victoria's and Beverley's eyes. Catherine turned to her father, Juri and said, "Dad, we wanted to wait until next week to tell you at your birthday, but I think Chet will forgive me if I let the secret out now, as my morning sickness seems to have progressed to evening sickness too... we're pregnant!"

Suddenly the whole house erupted in the sounds of pure joy and ec-static high fiving and back slapping! Juri rushed to hug his daughter and son-in-law. Thomas opened some champagne while waiting his turn and Malcolm looked on in happiness for the entire family. He intrinsically knew this new event would take his meetings with the young expectant couple into a completely new direction.

The Money Moral

Never look a gift horse in the mouth – especially if it comes from the Taxman. Use the TFSA to park money you will need in your future; then multiply the riches by funding every family member's plan. Think TFSA first to build, grow and preserve family wealth.

Quickie Tax Quiz

1. How is TFSA contribution room different from RRSP contribution room?

2. How does the TFSA facilitate family income splitting?

3. What happens to TFSA accumulations when one spouse dies?

Check out the answers in *Family Tax Essentials Portal* at www.knowledgebureau.com.

Such is Life:
When Babies Arrive, Benefits Flow

Chet and Catherine's impending parenthood was punctuated by so many firsts: Catherine's first maternity clothes; Chet's first toolkit for the assembly of the crib; and their new mutual worry about the future.

Baby had put a completely different perspective on their Wealth Purpose, and their journey for achieving it together. It was an interesting new phenomenon they shared, apparently, with the prospective grandparents: suddenly, the Family Wealth Purpose included concern not just about their own comfortable lifestyles, but that of the new, future generation.

Research, bears this out. It is not uncommon for one generation – the baby boomers, usually – to provide financial support for their adult children or aging parents. In the U.S., for example, one in five of these families are sharing a home with these other adults,[1] all of which can impact the number of detours a well thought-out Wealth Purpose can run into. Even more surprising is that four out of five investors provide financial support to other adults in their circle and, in turn, worry about the long term financial care required by those dependants.

They help in a number of different ways, paying for minor expenses for example, or funding education or mortgages. They also take care of their grandchildren, as both of Chet and Catherine's parents were excited to do, and that comes with a financial outlay as well.

Funding an education for children and grandchildren is very important to a family's Wealth Purpose. The total return on the investment

---

[1] 2013, UBS Investor Watch, UBS Financial Services, Inc., a subsidiary of UBS AG.

of a university or college education is significant. Having a high school diploma is important, but those with a college education earn 44% more; those with a university degree earn 85% more.[2] But education is expensive. Average undergraduate tuitions have risen in Canada recently; an increase of 16% in just five years. It's never too early, with these trends, to start saving for a child's education.

The reality for most families is that in the expensive consumption years are the very same ones in which they are acquiring and paying off mortgages and power-saving for their children's futures. That is all more difficult when the cost of living is rising around you.

The cost of total expenditures by average households in Canada, for example, increased by 4.7% recently, over the year before, to $79,000. For couples with children that number was $81,600.[3] Everything, it seems is going up in price: food costs increased 3.3% (more than restaurants at 2.7%); shelter increased by 3.6% and transportation by 7.4%. Health care costs rose, too, by 4.1%. The cost of personal income taxes keeps rising, too, at least for taxpayers in higher income brackets.[4]

What families need most in the expensive child-rearing years is cash flow, after taxes.

Having a sound Tax Strategy is a critical component of planning that falls right to the bottom line in a family budget. Catherine and Chet's TFSA deposits would be a good place to go in emergencies, as they could replace the deposits without losing their contribution room. However, they hated to do so, given the power of the tax free growth they would interrupt in that case.

Catherine and Chet were about to find out there are lots of tax preferences and social benefits to tap into when baby comes, as long as individual and family net income levels are below certain thresholds. The prospective new parents had a particularly eye-opening meeting the next time they visited with their accountant.

Malcolm delighted in asking Catherine about her growing baby

---

[2] Conference Board of Canada, Return on Investment of Tertiary Education, 2015

[3] Statistics Canada Survey of Household Spending, 2013, published January 22, 2015

[4] Federal Budget, April 21, 2015

bump. She was so excited! Chet, on the other hand, took his father-hood very seriously. He seemed preoccupied with the financials; worried about whether they could give their family all the advantages. It was a typical reaction for a new dad, and Malcolm used his experience and professionalism to help Chet understand his options better.

After a brief cup of coffee to catch up, he ushered the couple into the boardroom and proceeded to write three main titles on the white board in front of him:

REFUNDABLE CREDITS	DEDUCTIONS	NON-REFUNDABLE CREDITS

"You might recall that we discussed some time ago the reasons why we file a tax return: to calculate the correct amount of taxes for the previous calendar year; to pay any balance due or apply for a refund of overpayments and lastly, to tap into any refundable tax credits the government has available for your circumstances."

Malcolm turned to Catherine next. "Your return will change significantly once baby comes. You will likely be the one to claim the deductions and refundable credits; while Chet will claim the non-refundable amounts in most cases." He then refreshed the couple on the provisions they could count on when baby arrived.

The Federal Refundable Credits – The Canada Child Benefit and the GST/HST Credit. "When you have the baby, you'll probably find an application form for the Canada Child Benefit with your discharge at the hospital. Don't forget to complete this form. These social benefits can be quite lucrative, but they are based on net family income on the tax return; that is, both of your Line 236 amounts together. If your combined income in the last tax year is under about $30,000, you will qualify for the full amounts payable. If not, you may in the future, should your income drop," Catherine confirmed she be taking time off. "Another way to reduce net income is with an RRSP deduction. We'll do some 'what if' scenarios to determine if any refundable benefits will result together with the tax reductions."

He went on to remind Chet and Catherine never to miss filing a tax return. "I don't expect you'll ever be in this situation you two, but you should know that no- or low-income adults in most Canadian families should always file a tax return every year to receive their refundable tax credits like the GST/HST and CCB Credits. Also know that various provinces also offer tax form-based credits or monthly income supplements which are paid to low-income Canadians according to the net income reported on their returns."

Malcolm then emphasized an important principle about using any "baby bonuses" received from government redistributions: "The money received from these refundable tax credits can provide a great way to save for a child's future education. Open a separate bank account in the name of each of your children when they are born and deposit this money into them. Any resulting earnings are going to be taxed in your child's hands, and that is the first form of family income splitting you can participate in."

Catherine was expecting to work part-time out of her home office once the baby was six months old. "Will we still get the Canada Child Benefit?" It was a good question. "You will get a reduced credit," said Malcolm. "You'll be able to claim your child care expenses as a deduction and that can make a big difference in the size of your net income. Let's take a closer look at the rules." He turned to the second category on the board.

Child Care Deductions. "Parents who claim babysitting expenses will be happy with the increased child care expense deduction, effective the 2015 tax year," Malcolm explained to Catherine and Chet. "The maximum dollar amounts that can be claimed recently increased by $1,000 for each child. They are claimed by the lower income earner in general. For children under the age of 7, a maximum amount of $8,000 can be claimed, but this is only one factor."

"Other limitations are what you actually paid, and 2/3 of your actively earned income. There may be weekly maximums as well, depending on whether you are going to school, or are a higher income earner. For children who are disabled and eligible for the Disability Tax Credit the maximum claimable deduction is $11,000. I will worry about getting it right on form T778, you just have to provide me with the receipts, okay? These expenses are often audited and I want to be sure that, for you, it's nothing but smooth sailing with the CRA."

Chet and Catherine couldn't agree more. "Okay, we will save the receipts if you take care of calculating all of this for us, Malcolm," Catherine winced. "Deal," was the reply. "But what's important is what you do with that much bigger tax refund I will try to find for you, while claiming all the tax credits you are entitled to."

The conversation turned to Schedule 1 of the federal tax return next, where all of these elusive non-refundable credits seemed to reside. Malcolm pointed to the next subject on the white board.

Non-refundable Tax Credits: Malcolm referred to an appendix of various credits that reduce taxes payable; amounts for children who are disabled, the costs of adopting a child, amounts for tuition, education, textbooks and student loans, medical expenses and the costs of enrolling children in arts classes. There was even a tax credit for the costs of using public transit.[5] Tax software would claim most of these amounts automatically but receipts would be required when an out-of-pocket expense occurred.

"Here's the principle when it comes to cash flow planning with these boutique tax credits: use them before you lose them!" Malcolm was adamant about this. "I really try to dig for every tax credit I can find for your family because this generates new cash flow by way of a bigger tax refund. New governments often tinker with these tax benefits. We'll identify how much they increase your tax refund, adjust your tax withholdings if possible based on your RRSP savings and the amount of your child care expenses and then talk about investing any refund wisely in your children's education if you can."

It seemed to Catherine that she had just felt a little flutter inside her growing belly... was it her imagination or was this baby already moving? Catherine reached over to take her husband's hand and squeezed it. She was really happy.

The Money Moral

Tax filing is more complicated for families with children, but a sound Tax Strategy can relieve the financial stress most young families face. Maximizing government benefits available for families with children is an opportunity not to be squandered. If you qualify to receive money, save it for future needs, including education funding.

---

[5] See Essential Family Tax Facts in Part 7

Quickie Tax Quiz

1. Which parent would normally claim child care expenses?

2. What are the limitations on claiming child care expenses for a child under 7?

3. How can the Child Tax Benefit be invested without paying taxes on the income earned?

   Check out the answers in *Family Tax Essentials Portal* at www.knowledgebureau.com.

FUNDING EDUCATION COSTS
WITH THE RESP

It truly takes a village of financial support to help keep students out of a lifetime of debt. It was one of the issues that was keeping Chet awake at night. His blissful wife made sure his hand was on her tummy today when the baby's more obvious – and powerful – kicks began. It made everything so real... they were truly three now!

The next day, Chet's father was helping Chet think through all the possibilities for financial peace of mind. "The RESP or Registered Education Savings Plan is a good savings vehicle for parents to consider, because it comes with a government "sweetener'," he began.

"That's good dad, because I have been reading up on the cost of education and we are going to need all the help we can get!" Chet was consumed with the cost of the professions in particular. Dentistry, pharmacy, medicine and law were the professions with the highest undergraduate tuition fees in Canada, but masters of business education programs were the most expensive.

"Don't worry son. There are lots of ways for our family to embrace the challenge," he said with his sage and reassuring voice. "The RESP is one savings bucket that can come close to covering the costs of tuition." The two men discussed the details and virtues, as well as pitfalls to the RESP.

"Contributions to an RESP are made with after-tax dollars, Chet. To clarify, just like the TFSA, there is no tax deduction allowed when you invest money into an RESP. But the funds attract tax-deferred investment income. This will ultimately be tax free if our grandchild goes to school and withdraws the funds when they have little or no income."

"That's good, Dad," Chet responded, wondering how much he should contribute each year.

"There is actually no annual contribution limit, son, and a lifetime maximum contribution of $50,000 can be made for potential students under the age of 31. But even if you win the lottery, it's best not to contribute the $50,000 maximum in a lump sum. "

"Why?" asked Chet. His father explained that the RESP contribution also attracts participation from the federal government by way of that 'sweetener' he mentioned before. "It's called the Canada Education Savings Grant (CESG). For each beneficiary, this is 20% of your annual contribution, up to $2,500, to a maximum of $500 per year."

"I see, that's great," said Chet. "Therefore, it's best to contribute annually to maximize the grant, and start maximizing the tax-deferred earnings."

"Yes, but you could contribute in two-year cycles. If you have unused grant room from a missed prior year, you can receive a CESG of up to $1,000, when you contribute up to $5,000 in the current year."

"How much is the maximum amount the government will put towards the fund?" Chet wanted to make sure he anticipated the funds that could be received and their potential to compound.

"The maximum lifetime CESG is $7,200, and beneficiaries qualify for the grant until the end of the calendar year in which they turn 17. However, you must start saving in the RESP before the end of the calendar year in which the beneficiary turns 15 to be eligible for the grant," his father explained.

He also mentioned to Chet that a family RESP plan allows parents to name more than one beneficiary. "This must be someone related by blood or adoption, and under the age of 21, but we can ignore this age limit when funds are transferred from one plan to another," he noted. "Chet, your mother and I want you to know that we'd like to open an RESP for our grandchild and begin the process of saving for his or her future."

Chet was overwhelmed by his parents' generosity. "Thank you so much, Dad! But what ultimately happens to the money if, let's say, our child doesn't go to university?"

His father doubted very much that this would be the case. Their family village would encircle the child with opportunities to make the right choices in education and training. "If all goes as planned, our grandchild will attend post-secondary school. The CESG and its investment earnings, which have been accumulating on a tax-deferred basis along the way, will be withdrawn as Education Assistance Payments (EAPs). These amounts must be reported in income by our young scholar, and because students often have little or no income, the EAPs are often tax free or subject to very little tax cost," he said.

"What kinds of costs will the money fund? Are there restrictions?" His father, of course, knew the answers. Many of his clients had been curious too, over the years. "The maximum amount of EAPs is $5,000 until the student has completed 13 consecutive weeks in a qualifying education program at a post-secondary educational institution," he said. "Now you only need to be at school for 3 weeks if the student is studying abroad. But for anyone else, once the 13 weeks have been completed, there is no limit to the amount that may be withdrawn from the plan."

"That's good to know, Dad. I like that flexibility," said Chet. "So if I understand this correctly, there are no restrictions on how the EAPs are actually spent so long as the student is enrolled in a qualifying educational program for that minimum of 13 weeks."

Thomas agreed and the two went on to calculate the rates of returns they would require to ensure their future young lawyer or doctor would be funded by this terrific savings plan.

The Money Moral

Leverage the dollars government is prepared to give to important life events, like saving for your child's education. Why leave the RESP opportunity on the shelf, when the government is prepared to give contribute 20% of your investment to grow the education pot faster? Talk it over with your tax and investment advisors.

Quickie Tax Quiz

1. Why is it not a good idea to put the maximum $50,000 contribution into an RESP even if you have the cash to do so?

2. What is the maximum amount of Canada Education Saving Grant that can be accumulated for a child?

3. How do you ensure that the maximum CESG is earned?

   Check out the answers in *Family Tax Essentials Portal* at www.knowledgebureau.com.

MAXIMIZING WEALTH POTENTIAL:
FAMILY INCOME SPLITTING

Using a TFSA and an RESP as core investment opportunities within the family are good and acceptable ways to transfer both capital and income from higher earners to lower earners. For anyone with a lifetime Wealth Purpose, it's really imprudent not to take advantage of them, because the *Income Tax Act* affords very few opportunities to transfer assets and income without penalty.

People who want to reach their Wealth Purpose sooner, will maximize their Wealth Potential deliberately and consistently along the way. They don't waste money. They, in fact, find a job for every single dollar they earn, in order to build on and preserve its value. They also carefully measure their progress, making sure they account for real dollars – after taxes. Why is that so important?

It's possible to overstate how much you have to spend
by failing to account for taxes.

Within the context of a family, every Tax Strategy that works for one member of the family, has the potential to work for others, therefore exponentially propelling the economic power of the family unit into the financial stratosphere.

When families start strategizing about Family Net Worth, instead of individual Personal Net Worth, true multi-generational wealth planning can take place. The big advantage is this: the family unit loses the economic restrictions that one human lifeline provides and gains the power of the time value of money over many lifelines. Instead of planning for 60 years, in other words, a Family Wealth Purpose may span 90 years, for the youngest to the oldest stakeholder in the family. The types of decisions that can be made in that scenario, are obviously quite different.

> *When income and capital is distributed in the family,*
> *you simply get better after-tax results.*

The Taxman knows this. For these reasons, we have the Attribution Rules in the *Income Tax Act*. These rules deny you the opportunity to split income in the family when you transfer assets from the higher earner to the lower-earning spouse or minor children.

If you do attempt to transfer assets in this way, any earnings from the transferred property are "attributed" back to you, which means, you report the income. Malcolm was discussing this concept with Thomas, Beverley, Chet and Catherine. The family was trying to understand their options in doing some multi-generation planning, now that the birth of the new baby was so near. Malcolm thought it best to explain the concepts using an example, which he outlined to the two families:

"Consider our fictional taxpayer, John, who transfers $75,000 to his wife Sue, to invest in the stock market. John has a very high income and wants Sue to be able to report future capital gains, because her income is very low. Unfortunately, John will have to report those gains because of the Attribution Rules."

"Now, let's say John transfers $75,000 to his 15-year-old son, Jason. This money earns interest, dividends and on disposition, a capital gain. In this case, John must report the interest and dividends until his son turns 18. However, there is an exception in the Attribution Rules when it comes to capital gains earned by minors: Jason may at any time sell the shares and the resulting gain is taxed in his hands."

"In another example, my fictional client May is 79, and very ill. May has an adult daughter, Summer. May wants to put her daughter's name on her bank accounts so she can look after her affairs if she becomes incapacitated. May, will, however, continue to report the income from those accounts, even though her daughter's name appears on the account and on the T5 slip."

"Confused? Many people are," he said. "For these reasons, you need to know some of the tax rules. So, to begin, if one spouse transfers property to the other spouse for investment purposes, resulting income from the investment is taxed in the hands of the transferor.

But there are some interesting exceptions to these rules."

Malcolm pulled out an example again. "Here's one with our favorite investment topic, the TFSA. Terri earned $45,000 last year while her husband Jack was a full-time student with no taxable income. Terri gave Jack $5,500 to contribute to his TFSA this year. So long as the funds remain in the TFSA, no taxes are payable on the earnings either by Jack or by Terri. Parents or grandparents can also gift money to their adult children's or grandchildren's TFSA."

Malcolm's audience of four was enthralled by the potential! But there was another important exception to the Attribution Rules, one that both Chet and Thomas would use: spousal RRSP contributions.

"Contributions to a spousal RRSP, including the earnings on those contributions become income of the spouse to which they are gifted, three years after the last contribution is made to a spousal RRSP. Otherwise a portion of the withdrawals will be taxable to the contributor." He provided an example to make this a bit clearer:

"Quentin contributed $5,000 to a spousal RRSP for Rosie over the past two years. This year, Rosie took $6,000 out of the plan. Only the income attributed to the first contribution year can be reported by Rosie. Quentin must report the rest."

Thomas now wanted to jump in with an exception of his own: earnings from non-registered accounts. "Normally any income earned on money I transfer to my stay-at-home spouse during the child rearing years will be taxed back in my hands. But, income resulting from transactions in which bona fide 'inter-spousal' loans are drawn up for the transfer of the capital can be reported by my spouse. However, I must charge interest at the prescribed rate of interest or more and my spouse actually has to pay me at least once a year during the year or within 30 days after the year end – that's January 30, not the 31st."

"Fascinating," said Beverley. She had to admit to Thomas on more than one occasion that she normally was not too interested in any of this financial stuff. At any rate, he always took care of it. But Bev knew she had to *Know More*... just in case something ever happened to Thomas.

"Let's now take a look at what happens to profits from your spouse's investment in your business, Catherine," Malcolm teased deliberately as Catherine groaned, "... well, assuming that may happen sometime in the future, right?" Chet smiled and grimaced as his wife punched his arm.

"Here's what you need to know: only income from property is subject to the Attribution Rules; business income is not. That essentially means one spouse may give the other funds to start a business and, so long as they are not a partner in the business, the business income is taxed only to the business owner – in this case, the lower earning spouse."

Malcolm stepped up to the white board to make some notes about another case he was working on, disclaiming again that all numbers and names were fictitious, but that the concepts were relevant to their discussions.

"Anne gave her husband, Bruno, $25,000 to start a business a couple of years ago. The business finally made a profit of around $20,000 last year. The $20,000 income is reported as Bruno's income and will not attributed back to Anne even though she provided the funds to start the business. That's great news for the couple, as the income taxes Bruno will need to pay are much lower – he's in the lowest tax bracket while she's in the highest. The family unit, wins with thousands more in cash flow."

"One more important thing to know," Malcolm concluded, "Income earned after any assets are transferred by a deceased taxpayer will be reported as income of the beneficiary. Attribution Rules do not apply to the deceased taxpayer... sort of a 'final farewell' break from the Taxman, right Thomas?"

"Yes, you're right, Malcolm," Thomas chuckled. "But let's zero in on Attribution relating to minor children, since my grandson or granddaughter will likely receive some gifts of money and property along the way from all of us." Malcolm invited Thomas to stay on his feet and do some explaining.

"When it comes to the transfer of money to minors, the rules are similar, but at the same time, contain some advantages not available to spouses. Any income in the form of dividends and interest will be attributed back to the transferor. But here's the important difference: capital gains generated by the investment will be taxed in the hands of the minor."

Malcolm couldn't help himself... he had to jump in with a fabulous example to illustrate Thomas's point.

"My friend, let's call him Evan, has given 100 shares in The Walt Disney Company to his grandson David each year on his birthday. While David is under age 18, all of the dividends earned on those shares are attributed back to Evan, who must report the income. But, as soon as David turned 16, he sold the shares to buy a car. The capital gain on the sale of those shares was reported by David as his income and not attributed back to Evan. Evan, by the way, was the first person to ride in David's new car."

The delegation chuckled as coffee was refreshed and communications were checked. The conversation turned to Chet and Catherine, who already understood that any income earned on the investment of Canada Child Benefits in an account held in trust for their child would be reported and taxed to the child. Because of the Basic Personal Amount, or tax-free zone available to each taxpayer in Canada, this meant no taxes until income exceeded about $11,500.

"But babies can earn lots of money," Malcolm said. "Let's say your little one is a famous baby model and earns thousands of dollars in royalties from the pictures you take, Catherine. As long as you invest these 'own source' earnings in his or her name alone, untainted by birthday money or other money received from these doting grandparents, the resulting earnings are properly taxed in the hands of the baby."

"And by the way," he added, "we would be filing a tax return for that baby to report the income and in the process, creating unused RRSP contribution room which we would carry forward to use as a deduction to reduce income, once the child's income becomes taxable. This could happen if your child worked in your business, Catherine. You could pay your child for the work done – perhaps clerical work, distribution of marketing materials, and so on. The wage costs would be deductible to you and reportable on the child's return, providing what you paid him or her was reasonable and necessary."

Beverley spoke up at this point. "Are there any restrictions on the type of property that can be transferred or loaned to Chet and Catherine, our adult children? "

"Good question," Malcolm said. "The answer is no. All resulting income will be taxed in their hands. However, if you give your assets to your adult children, you personally may have a tax consequence on the transfer, because any increase in the value of the asset must be reported as a capital gain. I would help you with that before the transfer to make sure we all understood the tax consequences."

Malcolm then went on to describe an avoidance transaction CRA would frown upon. "Now, if the tax department believes the main reason for the loan to Chet and Catherine was to reduce or avoid taxes on your return, you'd have a problem. I recently took on a new client to help with this exact situation."

Malcolm went on to describe the circumstances. "The income of mom, in this case, was in a high tax bracket. Her son Jeffrey's was in the lowest tax bracket. He had been working as a waiter while going to college, but recently, Jeffrey dropped out. He currently lives at home in his parent's basement. With no income, these two parents have provided Jeffrey with spending money while he figures out what he wants to do with his life."

"Mom decided it would be a good idea to temporarily transfer to Jeffrey, the portion of her stock portfolio that is paying dividends. She thought that Jeffrey could then use the mostly tax-free dividends for spending money. Otherwise, her marginal tax rate on the same dividends was much higher. CRA would see this as a tax avoidance maneuver and attribute the dividend income back to mom."

This was a good time to call it a day. Chet and Thomas shook hands with Malcolm; the ladies had hugs for him. Malcolm truly was their most trusted financial advisor. It was comforting to know he was in their corner, not just for individual tax planning advice, but in collaboration with the needs of their growing family.

The Money Moral

Families have a tremendous opportunity to combine their time and money to build family wealth. Taxes are a major wealth eroder. Whenever a legitimate opportunity arises to split income or transfer assets to lower earners, who then have the opportunity to report income, apply losses or report future capital gains, the family will win financially by increasing its net worth.

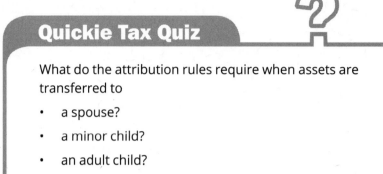

Quickie Tax Quiz

What do the attribution rules require when assets are transferred to

- a spouse?

- a minor child?

- an adult child?

Check out the answers in *Family Tax Essentials Portal* at www.knowledgebureau.com.

CLAIMING FAMILY
MEDICAL
EXPENSES

Catherine's pregnancy was going really well. It was so exciting to think the baby would arrive in less than 3 months. Chet had his heart set on a boy, of course, and they agreed he could choose the name for his son in that case. Catherine had a pretty good idea of the names she would prefer for her daughter, but liked to tease Chet with suggestions he'd roll his eyes at.

One night, though, Catherine had some unusual, sharp pain. She was unable to walk and Chet called the ambulance. It turned out to be a very early false labour, putting everyone on the alert for the potential of a premature baby. The young couple was shaken, but calmed by their very capable doctor, who advised bedrest for the remainder of the pregnancy.

When the $600 ambulance bill arrived, Chet paid it immediately, but called Malcolm to find out if it will be usable on his taxes at all. Malcolm reminded him that only the portion unreimbursed by his medical plan at work would be claimed on the personal tax return.

But, as usual, Malcolm over-delivered and exceeded expectations. With Chet's permission, he showed up at the door with a gigantic, stuffed toy; a panda bear and a gorgeous flower arrangement to cheer Catherine up. She was delighted, but still very fatigued. Malcolm and Chet went to the kitchen to make some tea and give Catherine a bit of time to rest.

"I would love to know more about what medical expenses can be claimed on the tax return, Malcolm. It's something I think we should know; can't image this is the last time we might transport someone to the hospital." Chet knew it would take a bit of an edge off his worry about Catherine and the baby to listen to Malcolm describe the rules to him.

"Indeed, medical expenses are one of my favorite subjects because everyone has a question about them," Malcolm smiled. "They qualify for a non-refundable credit on Schedule 1, Chet, and you will be able to claim total expenses for your immediate family (spouse and dependent children) for *any 12-month period* ending in the year. This means, that if your biggest medical expenses occurred between June last year and May this year that's the period you'll claim on this year's return. You'll save the rest of your receipts for next year."

But, there was a catch; which Malcolm explained next: "Unfortunately, many higher earners can't actually claim their medical expenses. That's because the claim for medical expenses is reduced by 3% of net income to a set maximum, which is just over $2,000. This maximum is reached when net income exceeds approximately $73,000."

An example came next: "Assume your net income is $60,000, and your medical expenses are $1,500. There will be no claim because 3% of your net income is $1,800 and that exceeds your total medical expenses."

"In this case," advised Malcolm, "you would want to try to group medical expenses for the family together to get over that $1,800 threshold to make a claim. Another strategy is to have the lower earning spouse make the claim for medical expenses. Approximately 20% to 25% of the allowable amount will offset any taxes owed. The real dollar value of this claim will depend on your province of residence."

"So, that means Catherine should claim the medical expenses, as her income is lower." Malcolm agreed with Chet here, pointing out that if Catherine was not taxable, the receipts should be carried forward for a possible future claim.

"Grouping together expensive dental or eyeglass costs, or treatments and devices not covered in a group health plan over a two year period can often can make a claim worthwhile," he said. "But, if your best 12 month period ends in December, make some of those dental or eye glass appointments before year end to get a tax refund sooner."

The two discussed what other medical expenses are claimable; but

Malcolm promised an email would follow with a list. Catherine was fast asleep by this time. She seemed to be exhausted.

An hour later, Chet turned down the lights and read the note from Malcolm: "Don't worry so much, Chet. Catherine looks wonderful and the baby will be fine, I am sure. Take it easy on yourself. For your distraction, here is the list of allowable medical expenses, courtesy of the CRA. It included everything from lists of types of medical practitioners to whom payments could be made, to ambulance fees and Blue Cross premiums."[1]

His email concluded with a reminder that the cost of training and care of service animals to help an individual manage severe diabetes, together with the cost of travel for the individual to attend a facility that trains such animals qualifies, too.

"Really couldn't have guessed that dogs could qualify as tax deductions!" thought Chet as he chuckled. Then he remembered… Malcolm would have surely corrected him. Medical expenses weren't a deduction, but rather a non-refundable tax credit.

Chet learned also that home modifications would qualify too – a good bit of trivia for his next fishing trip with the guys. For sure his lawyer friends wouldn't know that the incremental costs of building or modifying a new home for a patient who is physically impaired would qualify for the tax reduction. Nor would they know that you could double dip with these expenses – they also qualify for the Home Accessibility Tax Credit. Malcolm was giving him lots of new ammunition.

The Money Moral

It pays to hunt down medical expenses and claim them over the best 12-month period **ending in the tax year**. There are numerous out-of-pocket expenses ranging from batteries for hearing aids to driveway alteration costs for disabled family members that qualify.

---

[1] See page 160 for the list.

Quickie Tax Quiz

1. Why are medical expenses often more lucrative if claimed by the lower-income spouse?

2. What is the maximum period over which medical expenses can be claimed in a given tax year?

3. If an expense qualifies to be claimed as a medical expense and also qualifies to be claimed under the Home Accessibility Tax Credit, which claim should be made?

Check out the answers in *Family Tax Essentials Portal* at www.knowledgebureau.com.

SPECIAL PROVISIONS
FOR CAREGIVERS

The blessed aged add richness to our lives, but often their caregivers require more help. Catherine's mom and dad had recently considered the probability that Victoria's mother, Ina, may soon need more assistance in a personal care home. It was a heartbreaking thought. Ina was always so beautiful and feisty. A very successful entrepreneur in her day, she now was suffering early onset Alzheimer's disease.

There are 5.4 million caregivers in Canada, and close to 60% of them give more than 10 hours of care per week – 40 hours per month – primarily to females over the age of 85 who have a serious illness like dementia. According to a recent study by Statistics Canada, these caregivers, are worried, overwhelmed and anxious, and two thirds of them incur financial consequences as well: non-reimbursed expenses of $500 to over $2,000 per year in relation to the care they give.

Catherine asked Malcolm to provide some information to her parents. They chatted via Skype. Catherine's mom had found a job at the museum, which she absolutely loved. It gave her the opportunity to use her creative skills and meet new friends in their new city. The weather on the west coast was spectacular too. Her shades hid the sadness in Victoria's eyes. She was thinking about moving gramma into their home to begin with, and see what happens from there. She loved her mother dearly and hated to see her deteriorating health.

Malcolm took the lead in the conversation and his professionalism kick-started the necessary financial discussions. "There are some new opportunities that provide relief to caregivers, like you, Victoria, which you will be happy to know about. As of January 2016, the maximum benefit period for claiming Compassionate Care Benefits from Employment Insurance increased from six weeks to six months. Should you need to leave your job to take care of gramma, there will be at least some economic consideration for you. Your time off can be used to provide psychological or emotional support; arrange for care for your mom by a third party or for you to directly provide and participate in the actual care." Malcolm would later embellished on the details in an email, copied to Catherine, Victoria and Juri.

"To qualify," he wrote, "there must be a 40% or more decrease in income, you must have accumulated 600 insured hours in the last 52 weeks and there is a two-week waiting period. For 2016 the maximum assistance was $537 per week and so a maximum benefit of $13,962 over 26 weeks is possible. "

He also embellished on the Caregiver Amount, a non-refundable tax credit on the tax return. "Should gramma come to live in the same home with you, Victoria, I will adjust the amount claimable with the amount of gramma's net income. The doctor must complete Form T2201. Your possible credit is reduced and then phased out completely if gramma's income exceeds just over $22,000. The credit brings to you a maximum of $1,000 in tax relief against federal taxes payable together with a provincial benefit."

"As well you can claim a maximum of $2,000 to move gramma into your home. You can also claim the lesser of $5,000 and 20% of the cost of a van if you decide to buy one, and adapt it for a wheelchair."

"I was mentioning the Home Accessibility Tax Credit to Chet last week," Malcolm continued in his email. "It's computed as 15% of a maximum of $10,000 in costs incurred to make a home more accessible to the disabled. Allowable renovation costs may be claimed for these purposes as well as under medical expenses."

Malcolm then went on to describe one of the more lucrative credits on the tax return: the *Disability Amount*. "This should be claimed on the return of the disabled adult; gramma in this case. If not needed, because income is too low, the amount can then be transferred to a supporting individual, for example, to you Victoria or Juri. It generally results in an additional real dollar return of around $2,000, depending on province of residence."

Therefore, claiming the *Caregiver Amount*, the *Home Accessibility Tax*

Credit and the *Disability Amount* for a seriously ill dependant with little income who lives with you, can bring thousands of real dollar benefits to supplement your cash flow in these difficult circumstances. "Check to see if you have the required insurable hours Victoria," Malcolm advised. "We can then monitor when to apply for further assistance from EI – which can be as high as $2,000 a month."

The Money Moral

The tax system can adequately compensate most people with taxable incomes for the cost of caring for their loved ones who are seriously ill.

Quickie Tax Quiz

1. What is the maximum duration of a claim for compassionate care for 2016?

2. The claim for the Caregiver Amount is reduced if the dependant has income of their own. At what income level is the Caregiver Amount eliminated?

3. What can be done if a dependant qualifies for the Disability Amount but does not have enough income to use this non-refundable tax credit?

   Check out the answers in *Family Tax Essentials Portal* at www.knowledgebureau.com.

TWO-PARENT FAMILIES WITH KIDS

Catherine gave birth to a beautiful little girl, Olivia Grace... and a little boy, Oscar Thomas. No one had expected little Oscar's arrival! No wonder Catherine had been so tired over her last couple of months. The babies were perfectly healthy and so adorable. Chet was over-the-top, overjoyed.

Life was going to be very busy, and Chet's Wealth Purpose would need to take a little detour. He was little worried how they would all fit into their home; clearly a larger one would be required in due course, but the advent of his instant "Million Dollar Family", caused Chet to bring focus to his process for financial peace of mind.

He spent some time thinking about his Wealth Potential, now that they were a family of four. Certainly he would take on new and more lucrative assignments at work. But he also knew that tweaking their financial activities a bit more, would make a big difference over the long run. He wrote down the following goals:

1. We won't waste money, we'll use it strategically to meet our goals.
2. We won't carry credit card debt – we'll pay it off every month.
3. We will power-save for our children's education, in separate accounts.
4. We will invest in a larger tax exempt principal residence.
5. We will work on building more equity in Catherine's business, so we can sell it in the future.
6. We will invest regularly through auto savings plans into the right buckets for emergencies and retirement.
7. We will measure the increase in our wealth after tax, to be sure we know our real dollar values.
8. We will do One Fun Thing every month to live a balanced life.

Chet high-balled his monthly after-tax budget at $5,800, after taxes. He was already investing $675 a month in his employer's pension plan, which came off his gross pay and had a great family health plan. In making his plans, he would assume that Catherine was staying at home with the babies for a while.

FAMILY INCOME SPLITTING	TFSA	RESP	RRSP	TAX EXEMPT HOME
Free: Save Canada Child Benefits in Trust for the Kids	Save $915 per month in each TFSA ($11,000/yr.)	Save $400 per month in RESPs (total $5000/yr. to get the 20% CESG)*	Save $800 per month in his & Spousal RRSP ($9,600/yr.)	Pay $1500 a month towards mortgage, home costs

* Chet's parents had promised to help with this one

It was going to be ambitious, but it was affordable. There would be enough left over for food, clothing and fun. Malcolm agreed it was doable, but, things would be tight for the family, especially if a large repair or other expense was necessary. "Let's do the tax math, Chet, to be sure you can afford this plan. We should do some year-end tax planning, too, to see if we can free up some cash flow for you to fund some of these money buckets. Let's consider this strategically in the context of your Wealth Purpose and Plan."

The two men revisited Chet and Catherine's financial priorities; reviewed prior filed returns and prepared their personal net worth statements. The family's finances were sound, and they had some options to work with because they had some cash on hand and some accrued gains in their non-registered investment portfolio. Malcolm came up with a three-part plan to enhance cash flow with tax savings:

SPEND TO SAVE TAXES	**INVEST TO SAVE TAXES**	**RECOVER OVERPAID TAXES**

Step 1 – Spend to Save. "Two non-refundable tax credits require your attention before year end, Chet. These include **charitable donations** and any **medical expenses** you may have incurred or will yet incur with the new babies."

It's important to donate generously before year end if you believe in giving back. "Do take advantage of the *First Time Donor's Super Credit*, available only in the period 2013 to 2017. Recall, I described this to you last year," Malcolm said. "The credit increases the regular donations credit from 15% to 40% of donations under $200 and from 29% to 54% for donations between $200 and $1,000. So, when you give $1,000 in cash to your favorite charity, you'll get back a federal credit of $512 – over half of it. Your provincial government will provide additional benefits."

"Once you don't qualify for the Super Credit any more, a more lucrative donation strategy can be executed when public securities you may own have appreciated in value. Consider transferring them directly to your favorite charity before Christmas. The transfer is tax exempt – that's the important part – but you'll also get a regular donation credit."

Malcolm really liked this opportunity and was excited as he explained it. "Consider the stocks your father recommended earlier this year. They have done really well. If you decided to sell the shares and then gift the cash to your favorite charity, half of the accrued capital gain of $10,000 would be included in income, attracting taxes of about $2,300 at a 46% marginal tax rate."

"Now here's the fantastic part: this taxable gain can be completely avoided with a transfer of the shares directly to the charity. The donation receipt would provide a further saving – about $5,800 federally plus the provincial tax savings of $2,200 in your case; an amount well over $8,300 in savings in this case. It's a gift that literally keeps giving back!"

Medical expenses can be claimed on the tax return as well, but Malcolm explained again that the total expenditures are reduced by 3% of net income up to a threshold of approximately $2,200. "Did you have more than that in unreimbursed medical expenses last year? Did Catherine? Will medical expenses this year be higher than last? Are there any other expensive costs to be incurred before year end – glasses, dental work, for example? If so, it may pay in tax savings to spend now, because medical expenses can be claimed in the best 12 month period ending in this tax year. Let's do the medical plan math once you've checked your receipts."

Step 2. Invest to Save. Malcolm wanted to be sure Chet and Catherine saved their money in the right "buckets" for their future; but he knew that saving would be more difficult now with starting a family and filling a home with everything the family needs. "Remember, the object is to invest more of the first dollars you earn, if possible, in a tax preferred investment," he counselled, "and then keep as many *dollars* invested for as long as possible. The RRSP is a good choice. Let's top it up and then have your employer reduce your withholding taxes to take this investment into account."

Malcolm checked Chet's Notice of Assessment from CRA to confirm the amount that could be contributed, based on prior year's actively earned income, the pension adjustment for the contributions in the employer-sponsored pension plan and the prior unused RRSP contribution room. "Another option: you could make a spousal RRSP contribution for Catherine, just as you have planned."

He reminded him that for eligible higher-earning investors, like Chet, lucrative tax reductions result from the RRSP deduction. "For example, let's assume again your marginal tax rate is 46%; investing $6,000 in an RRSP will result in an increased tax refund of $2,760. That's good money that can help fund one of the babies' RESP contributions or 25% or your TFSA contribution."

Malcolm smiled. He knew Chet was already on the same page with this type of planning. "Remember with your parents helping with the education funding, Chet, we can make sure the RESPs are set up and focus on investing your refund in next year's RRSP or in your tax exempt principal residence instead."

Step 3. Recover Overpaid Taxes. Chet was very interested in knowing that errors and omissions made on the tax return could be adjusted over a period of ten tax years. "Yes, it's possible for you to recover missed tax deductions and credits, but only for a ten-year period. That makes December 31 an important date, as one tax year always drops off," he learned. "This could significantly interrupt your wealth accumulation plans if you miss some important carry forward provisions, tax credits or a tax refund."

They knew that Malcolm was very thorough when it came to claiming all their deductions and credits, but he had only done one year of returns for them. Under the topic of "big ticket misses", Malcolm was passionate about two and he reminded Chet to review prior filed returns in case there were any errors in filing:

- *Unclaimed Capital Losses.* "It's always important to report any capital losses you may have missed claiming. They are lucrative, because prior year loss balances can reduce capital gains this year, or any time in the future in which capital gains are reported. This is a great way to recover tax previously paid on capital gains or reduce taxes on future gains throughout your lifetime," he advised.

- *Missed Carrying Charges.* "Did you know that interest paid on loans used to acquire assets with now-diminished values will continue to be deductible? What this means is that if you took out a $50,000 loan to invest in the stock market and the value of the securities dropped in half during the financial crisis, your interest costs on the original loan will still be deductible."

Chet smiled. He had had some heart-stopping moments back in 2008, as a rookie investor, but his investments had recovered. However, he did have a personal line of credit. He had borrowed against it to buy some shares a couple of years ago, but had not prorated the interest paid to account for this legitimate expense of investing.

Malcolm also asked whether he or Catherine had missed filing any returns in the past 10 years. "If so, we can catch up on filing any missing tax returns, which will provide a lucrative opportunity to recover refunds that could be owing to you. You'll also avoid paying penalties by filing missed returns before CRA asks you for them."

"Last, but not least, you will preserve unused RRSP contribution room, if you have the required earned income in the missed year. This can help you increase your future retirement income." They had covered this off when Malcolm first met Catherine and Chet and so the only adjustment would be to include the missed interest expenses on the line of credit. The year end plan was done; Chet would invest $7,000 now to earn close to $4,000 in tax savings and end up with $6,000 in his RRSP, too. It was a good day.

SPEND TO SAVE TAXES	INVEST TO SAVE TAXES	RECOVER OVERPAID TAXES
Make a $1,000 cash donation Tax Savings: $600	Make $6,000 RRSP contribution Tax Savings $2,760	Claim $1000 in missed carrying charges Tax Savings $460

"Will I have any new tax credit claims for the babies this year?" It was a great question from the proud new dad.

"Unfortunately, no," Malcolm responded. He explained that the non-refundable tax credit for children under 18 has been discontinued. "This means we can't reduce your tax withholdings. The only tax relief in sight for the babies is an enhancement to the refundable Canada Child Benefit, which is why we want to keep a close eye on the level of your net family income with an RRSP contribution for both you and Catherine. Once Catherine goes back to work, we'll be vigilant about claiming child care expenses too."

The Money Moral

There's lots you can do before year end to arrange your affairs within the framework of the law to pay the least taxes possible and ensure your happy financial journey into the new year, quite possibly to include a vacation, funded with your tax savings.

Quickie Tax Quiz

1. Who qualifies for the Donation Super Credit?
2. Why is it more lucrative to donate shares that have increased in value than to donate cash?
3. How can an investment in your RRSP help with your TFSA investment?

   Check out the answers in *Family Tax Essentials Portal* at www.knowledgebureau.com.

THE MONEY MORALS:
Family Tax Filing Milestones

Work with Real Dollars. Money is a tool to use to your strategic advantage. You've given every dollar a job; now focus on measuring income and wealth, after taxes. That's really important for a young family; especially at year end.

Tax Gifts are for Investors. Never look a gift horse in the mouth – especially if it comes from the Taxman. Use the TFSA to park money you will need in your future; then multiply the riches by funding every adult family member's plan. Think TFSA first to build, grow and preserve family wealth.

Compute the Value of Tax Credits and Deductions. Tax filing is more complicated for families with children, but a sound Tax Strategy can relieve the financial stress most young families face. Maximizing government benefits available for families with children is an opportunity not to be squandered. If you qualify to receive money, compute the real dollar value of those after-tax bonuses; then sock it away in the right buckets for future needs.

Plan to Leverage Education Savings Plans. Leverage the dollars government is prepared to give to important life events, like saving for your child's education. Why leave the RESP opportunity on the shelf, when the government is prepared to give contribute up to 20% of your investment to grow the education pot faster? Talk it over with your tax and investment advisors.

Split Income and Assets with the Family. Families have a tremendous opportunity to combine their time and money to build family wealth. Use lawful and legitimate opportunities to split income or transfer assets to lower earners, who then will report income, apply losses or report future capital gains in their hands. The family will win financially by increasing its net worth with this strategy.

Turn to the Tax System for Cash Flow When Health Changes. It pays to hunt down medical expenses and claim them over the best 12-month period ending in the tax year. There are numerous out-of-pocket expenses ranging from batteries for hearing aids to driveway alteration costs for disabled family members that qualify. It's a great supplement to cash flow in the face of rising medical costs.

Year End Planning Pays Off. There's lots you can do before year end to arrange your affairs within the framework of the law to pay the least taxes possible and ensure your happy financial journey into the new year, quite possibly to include a vacation, funded with your tax savings.

PROCESS CHART: Family Filing Milestones

These age-related tax milestones indicate a new or changed filing status; you might wish to ask your pro about new tax provisions that now will apply to you:

Milestone	Significance for Tax Preparation or Planning
Birth to age 7	Claim child care expenses and apply for enhanced Canada Child Benefits
	Claim non-refundable credits for dependent children under 18 who are disabled
	Claim Children's Fitness Tax Credit and Children's Arts Tax Credit available
	Claim Disability Amount for a disabled child
	Open bank account and deposit Canada Child Tax Benefit and gifts from non-residents – both escape the Attribution Rules
	Gift investments that produce capital-gains – Attribution Rules do not apply
	Open RESP savings accounts to earn up to $500 in Canada Education Savings Grants or Bonds
Ages 7-17	Claim for dependent children under 18 who are disabled
	Child care expense claim reduced but still possible
	Children's Fitness Tax Credit and Children's Arts Tax Credit available
	Canada Child Benefits reduced but still possible
	Create RRSP room by reporting all employment/self-employment
	Continue to invest in RESP; CESG eligibility ends at end of the year the child turns 17
	Continue to deposit Canada Child Benefits into untainted savings account

Age 18	File return so child receives GST/HST Credit starting the quarter after the 19th birthday CPP premiums become payable the month after the 18th birthday Canada Child Benefits end; Eligibility for amount for eligible dependant ends TFSA contribution room begins to accumulate
Age 19	GST/HST Credit becomes payable after turning 19 Post-secondary school bound: report RESP income, tuition/ education/ textbook amounts, student loan interest
Ages 20-30	Income splitting, RRSP spousal plans, TFSA First Time Home Buyers' Tax Credit may be utilized Use Home Buyers' Plan and Lifelong Learning Plan under RRSP
Age 49	Last year for earning of Registered Disability Savings Grants and Bonds
Ages 31 to 59	Peak productivity: RRSP and TFSA maximization; tax efficiency in non-registered savings; business start rules important Tax-wise employment negotiations important Charitable gift planning: annual updates required Parental care: Caregiver Amount, EI Compassionate Care Benefits, claim medical expenses, claim Home Accessibility Tax Credit
Age 60 plus	CPP early retirement (age 60 – 64), normal (age 65), or late retirement (age 66 – 70); apply to split income with spouse Withdrawals from RDSPs must begin after age 59 Retirement income sources change taxpayer profile Pension withdrawal planning; clawback zones; pension income splitting Transfer of property within the family OAS begins at age 65 (but may be delayed up to age 70) Age Credit Amount starting at age 65 Pension income splitting for RRSP/RRIF starting at age 65 Withdrawals from RRSP by age 71; make spousal RRSP contribution if spouse is under age 71 and you have contribution room Check tax instalment payment requirements Home Accessibility Tax Credit eligibility at age 65

CHECKLIST FOR CLAIMABLE MEDICAL EXPENSES

Eligible Amounts Paid to Medical Practitioners

- ☐ a dentist
- ☐ a medical doctor
- ☐ a medical practitioner
- ☐ an optometrist
- ☐ a pharmacist
- ☐ a psychologist
- ☐ a speech-language pathologist
- ☐ an osteopath
- ☐ a chiropractor
- ☐ a naturopath
- ☐ a therapeutist or therapist
- ☐ a physiotherapist
- ☐ a chiropodist (or podiatrist)

- ☐ a Christian science practitioner & certain psychoanalysts
- ☐ a psychologist
- ☐ a qualified speech-language pathologist or audiologist
- ☐ certain occupational therapists
- ☐ an acupuncturist
- ☐ a dietician
- ☐ a dental hygienist
- ☐ a nurse including a practical nurse whose full-time occupation is nursing
- ☐ a Christian science nurse
- ☐ an audiologist

Eligible Medical Treatments

- ☐ medical and dental services
- ☐ attendant or nursing home care
- ☐ ambulance fees
- ☐ transportation
- ☐ travel expenses (see below)
- ☐ eyeglasses
- ☐ guide dogs
- ☐ transplant costs
- ☐ alterations to the home for disabled persons (prescribed)
- ☐ lip reading or sign language training
- ☐ sign language services
- ☐ cost of training a person to provide care for an infirm dependant
- ☐ cost of deaf-blind intervening services
- ☐ reading services provided under a medical practitioner's prescription
- ☐ cost of drugs obtained under the Special Access Program

- ☐ for medical marihuana or marihuana seeds purchased from Health Canada, or a licensed person under Marihuana Medical Access Regulations (MMAR)
- ☐ therapy provided by a medical doctor, psychologist or occupational therapist for a patient who qualifies for the disability amount
- ☐ tutoring services for a patient with a learning disability or mental impairment
- ☐ drugs prescribed by a medical practitioner (see list above) and recorded by a pharmacist
- ☐ lab tests
- ☐ private health plan premiums, including group insurance premiums
- ☐ Blue Cross premiums including travel insurance costs

Medical Devices

- ☐ an artificial limb
- ☐ an iron lung
- ☐ a rocking bed
- ☐ a wheelchair crutches
- ☐ a spinal brace
- ☐ a brace for a limb

- ☐ an ileostomy or a colostomy pad
- ☐ a truss for a hernia
- ☐ an artificial eye
- ☐ a laryngeal speaking aid
- ☐ hearing aid
- ☐ an artificial kidney machine

PART 5 – GROW

PRIORITIZING:
GROWING YOUR MONEY BUCKETS

Retirement income adequacy, according to research by the Department of Finance,[1] "critically depends on three things: the tax assistance available for savings (RRSP versus non–RRSP), the timing of investments and the type of investment."

Most people can agree with that research. If taxes erode personal, business and investment performance, it's easy to understand that tax efficiency increases it. Skipping a few years in the savings cycle, exiting the markets at just the wrong time or starting late can also have a significant impact on the overall wealth that can be created to generate income for the future.

Those gaps and misses in your Wealth Potential can be overcome, however. When you plan income, investment distributions and withdrawals to stay clear of the next marginal tax bracket, you'll have a big win. Money will stay invested and taxes will remain deferred.

But it's in the last of the three critical components to retirement income adequacy – the type of investments you choose – that millions are made or lost. What you invest in and when is often more important than how much, as Chet and Catherine have discovered.

They have learned that they will easily surpass their retirement income needs and make up a lot of ground for the cash-strapped family years, when investing takes a back seat to mortgages and schooling. By consistently doing a few things right, like investing the maximum allowable amounts into a Tax Free Savings Account at the start of the year, Chet and Catherine can manage to meet their Wealth Purpose.

---

[1] Investment Performance and Costs of Pension and Other Retirement Savings Funds in Canada: Implications On Wealth Accumulation and Retirement, Dr. Vijay Jog, December 2, 2009

In addition, they can plan to supplement their now tax-free retirement income with two significant tax-free asset dispositions: the gains on the sale of a principal residence are completely tax free. In addition, should Catherine incorporate her business and later sell it, capital gains of up to more than $800,000 could qualify for tax-exempt status. These are the three ingredients that can make a multi-million dollar future, but they don't come without risk.

Yet, there are no guarantees. Governments can change can change TFSA contribution limits, thereby restricting the opportunity. The housing market could go down, rather than up, compromising equity in the tax exempt home. Owning, managing and safely selling a small business corporation takes money, skill and often, luck; not for everyone and not guaranteed. The self-made millionaire, however, hedges against uncertainty as a deliberate investor who diversifies holdings to manage risks that are beyond his or her control. He or she is also vigilant about risks that can be controlled: taxation and the cost of investing for example.

There are five important lifecycles you may wish to consider as you approach your planning:

Lifecycle	1	2	3	4	5
Age	0-17	18-35	36-54	55-70	71 plus
Life Purpose	Education	Home & Family	Career Building	Wealth Building	Retirement
Wealth Purpose	Learn	Accumulate	Grow	Preserve	Transition
Wealth Potential	Fund RESPs, Invest Child Benefits	Invest in TFSA, Create Income, Buy Residence, Insurance	Invest in TFSA, Maximize RRSP, Split income, Build Equity, Buy 2nd Residence	Invest in TFSA, Create income, Reduce Debt, Preserve Capital	Invest in TFSA, Create Income, Transition assets
Life Purpose	**Engage**	**Recreate**	**Build**	**Lead**	**Enjoy!**

Your Income Purpose. This is an era in which new marginal tax brackets are being created for taxpayers with incomes over $150,000. For many taxpayers the marginal tax rate paid on the next dollar earned is prohibitive – over 50% in many provinces. It's therefore most important to report only the right amount of "earned income" to fund consumption in the present, public and private pension plans in the future and keep the rest invested.

For older taxpayers, however, the opposite is true. Deliberately creating income to the top of a tax bracket can really pay off. The average income in Canada for an elderly male earner is $49,500; for the elderly female earner it's $40,300. For elderly couples, average household income is $56,700. In almost all of these cases, the income falls below or around the top of the lowest tax bracket. Pension income splitting gets good results as well. There is plenty of room to add taxable income before the highest marginal tax rates are reached.

However, should a surviving spouse or single senior pass away with a large lump sum left untaxed in his or her RRSP or RRIF, the remaining amounts must be included in income on the final return. There the money will be taxed at rates over 50%. It would have been much better to generate some taxable income along the way in lower brackets during this taxpayer's lifetime to avoid those high income brackets.

There is another powerful reason to keep a careful watch on the level of income generated for tax purposes; one that is more important for middle income earners as it is for the higher earners:

Middle earners are subject to clawbacks, and clawbacks are a form of tax.

The middle class, defined as individuals with incomes under $45,000, qualifies for income redistribution under income-tested benefits like the refundable Canada Child Benefit, the GST/HST Credit, as well as several non-refundable tax credits. But with every additional dollar earned above income-test ceilings, benefits and credits are reduced or eliminated. This results in high marginal tax rates for those families.

Consider that the Age Amount available to seniors over age 65 is reduced by 15% of income over approximately $35,000, which results in an increase in the marginal tax rate of 3% to 4% depending on the province. The Old Age Security clawback provides a 15% marginal tax rate increase on incomes in the clawback zones – between approximately $72,000 and $118,000.

The Canada Child Benefits are reduced by a marginal tax rate of between 6.8% and 16% depending on how many children the couple has. This occurs when family income exceeds $30,000 plus an addition increase of 3.1% to 8% when income exceeds $65,000.

In another example, the clawback of EI benefits contributes a 30% marginal tax rate on that income. When combined with taxes on all other forms of income, recipients of income-tested benefits face higher marginal tax rates in some cases than top income earners.

For these reasons, investing in tax sheltered investment vehicles like the RRSP are most important for those at lower income levels. . . the benefit of each tax dollar saved is higher, when net income levels can be reduced below clawback thresholds.

*The RRSP, therefore, trumps the TFSA if income falls
into clawback zones. Invest there first, if eligible.*

Maximizing Your Wealth Potential. Building your financial empire is about consistently putting your money to work for you in the right money buckets. There is an order of investing that's important to your ultimate wealth. Consider filling the following money buckets in your planning, indicating your priorities in Column 1:

PRIORITY	MONEY BUCKETS	PURPOSE
	TFSA	Worry-Proofing
	Canada Pension Plan	Employer Matched Retirement, Disability Benefits
	Employment Insurance	Manage risk to income
	Insurance	Manage risk to health and life
	Registered Pension Plan	Employer-sponsored – Embellishes Retirement
	RRSP	Manages Retirement Security
	RESP	Government-sponsored education Savings
	Principal Residence	Tax Exempt home equity
	Other financial investments	Build and preserve wealth
	Other non-financial investments	Build and preserve wealth

So to find homes for all your dollars, there are eight tax strategies you can employ to make every dollar work hard for you:

1 – Avoid Tax: This tax home is a Tax Free Savings Account (TFSA) or a tax exempt principal residence.

2 – Defer Tax: Here the tax home is a registered account. Examples include an RPP (Registered Pension Plan) an RRSP (Registered Retirement Savings Plan) or RRIF (Registered Retirement Income Fund) or an RESP (Registered Education Savings Plan).

3 – Earn Tax-Preferred Income: If your tax home is a non-registered account, earnings are reported annually. This can include interest, dividends and realized capital gains as well as other income, like foreign investment income, but it is the dividends and capital gains that attract lower marginal tax rates.

4 – Harvest Capital Losses: Give your capital losses a tax home. Always harvest them by reporting them on your tax return. They will offset capital gains of the current year, the previous three years or any year in the future in which you earn a capital gain, if there are no gains now.

5 – Blend Income and Capital for Tax-Preferred Cash Flow: Certain investments pay you a portion of your capital and a portion of your income for a better overall cash flow result. That tax home can increase your cash flow but not your taxes.

6 – Reduce Net Income: Give a tax home to refundable and non-refundable tax credits you may be eligible for. Any deduction leading to net income will help, but a particularly good one is the RRSP deduction if you have contribution room. You can invest throughout the year, and within 60 days of the year end, too.

7 – Split Income: While there are specific rules called the Attribution Rules that curtail family income splitting, there are exceptions that are legitimate, like investing in a Spousal RRSP or a TFSA for every adult family member. Finding tax homes for your high taxed dollars with other family members can average taxes downward for your family unit as a whole.

8 – Reinvest any tax refunds: Tax refunds behave best in a tax home like an RRSP or TFSA – which will conspire to build more wealth for you. Reducing expensive debt – like credit card balances with your tax refund, will also go a long way in meeting your Wealth Purpose.

The Money Moral

The tax homes you find for the dollars you earn will diversify your income sources, thereby averaging down the taxes you pay. That provides an interesting embellishment to your Personal and Family Net Worth Statements: an order in which to make your investments. So what comes first – the RRSP or the TFSA? It's going to depend on your age, your income sources and your commitment to your Wealth Potential.

BUILDING EQUITY WITH
YOUR FAMILY RESIDENCES

Chet and Catherine were quickly running out of room. Oscar and Olivia were happy, outgoing twins who had a way of accumulating friends, animals and toys wherever they went. A new four-bedroom home was definitely on the horizon, too, after Catherine told everyone her surprise: baby number three was onboard!

It was delightful, scary, and chaotic all at the same time, especially for Chet. Anytime those three circumstances crowded into their lives at the same time, the calming influence of Malcolm, the accountant seemed to be just the right solution.

Chet was doing very well at his law firm, but the hours were long. Catherine had continued her practice working from home and it too was going well, especially with Nanny Irena on board. She would now stay on with the family as a live-in; which is why they needed at least four bedrooms.

Malcolm had prepared cash flow projections for the family. He took this opportunity of a new move to educate Chet on the taxation of assets in Canada, starting with the principal residence.

"Under current tax rules, each household (assuming an adult taxpayer and spouse if there is one) can designate one principal residence to be tax exempt on sale or disposition at death or by transfer. But, a principal residence is classified to be 'personal-use property,' which means that any losses on disposition are deemed to be nil."

Chet cocked his head at that news. "That's right, Chet, if you lose money on the sale of your home, the loss is not claimable on the tax return."

A principal residence can include a house, cottage, condo, duplex, apartment, or trailer that is ordinarily inhabited by you or some family member at some time during the year. There is no minimum number of days for this purpose, either.

"There is more good news in these criteria," Malcolm said. "The principal residence also includes the housing unit and up to one-half hectare of subjacent property that contributes to the use of the housing unit as a residence. If the lot size exceeds one-half hectare, it may be included in the principal residence if it can be shown to be necessary for the use of the housing unit."

Chet hoped to be a ranch owner one day, so he pocketed that bit of tax trivia. But it appeared this dream would take some time as the twins, the new baby and Catherine were rather high maintenance at the moment.

"When do I report my gain on our last residence?" he asked.

"Even more good news," Malcolm's enthusiastic response blurted forward. "For tax compliance purposes, if you have had only one principal residence, used solely for personal use in the entire period you have owned it, no tax reporting is required at the time of disposition, even if a capital gain results. That gain is yours – completely tax free – no strings attached.

"Awesome!" Chet smiled in relief. But there was more to come. Malcolm knew that a second family home might be in the stars for Chet and Catherine. They would be taking over her parent's beautiful lakeside cabin.

"Where more than one property is owned, and the family uses both residences at some time during the year, the calculation of the principal residence exemption becomes slightly more difficult when one property is disposed of," Malcolm began to explain. "One property per year can be designated as a principal residence for the family, but no more."

So which one to choose? Malcolm explained that either property could be chosen as the principal residence, as long as the family lived in each at some time during the year.

"So I can live in my home in the city for 360 days and at the family cottage for four days and still claim a principal residence exemption for either home?" Malcolm nodded in the affirmative.

"We will generally want to claim as the tax exempt home, the property that appreciated the most in value. Fortunately, it is all sorted out on *Form T2091 – Designation of a Property as a Principal Residence by an Individual.*" Malcolm explained that this form helps you to calculate the exempt portion of any capital gain when one of two or more principal residences in the family are sold.

Chet was curious to see the form, and after careful review, gladly returned it to Malcolm. "Very glad you'll be completing this for us when the time comes, Malcolm!" The accountant smirked. He then went on to embellish on some important rules that would allow Chet and Catherine to use their real estate to earn money.

"Catherine is already writing off a portion of your home expenses for her home workspace," said Malcolm, "and that's a good way for you to supplement the costs of maintenance and repairs, mortgage interest, property taxes and so forth, with some tax savings."

Malcolm explained that when a taxpayer starts using a principal residence for income-producing purposes, for example as a rental or home office, "change of use" rules must be observed for tax purposes. "The fair market value of the property must be assessed in this case, because you are deemed to have disposed of the property and immediately reacquired it at the same fair market value, changing its classification from a personal-use property to an income-producing property. You will recall we did this the first time we filed for Catherine." Chet did remember that; as they had to confirm with an appraisal.

He also remembered that they reported no capital gain at that time. An election was made by Malcolm not to recognize the change in use of the property. Recognition of the change in use will be delayed until the time of sale of the property or when you rescind the election, Malcolm had told them. Any capital gain would then be accounted for. "But the capital gain would be considered to be nil, as long as the home is designated in each year as your principal residence," he told them. Again that complicated Form T2091 would be used to sort it all out.

In the meantime, Chet was thinking they could make some extra money by renting out the basement floor in their new home. They lived near the university and the suite was beautiful. He was sure they could find a suitable tenant to help cover the costs.

"If you rent a portion of your property; simply report rental income as usual," Malcolm offered. "You can still use it as a home workspace, too, and claim the expenses in the usual manner. However, it's very important that while your property is used for income-producing purposes of any kind, no Capital Cost Allowance (CCA) is used as a deduction, even for a small portion. This would compromise the principal residence exemption on that portion of the property, so you'll notice, I have not claimed this."

"What if I flip this residence to make some extra money, Malcolm? If the values increase, that may be a way to pay down some debt," Chet felt he had made a good investment and dreaded repeating any move with all his little people and their belongings; yet an opportunity to make a tax free gain was always a good one.

"Sure," said Malcolm. "During a real estate boom, the disposition of real property can be very lucrative, especially if you can earn one tax exempt gain after another with your principal residence."

"But, how often can you do that before it raises eyebrows at the CRA?" Chet wanted to know.

Malcolm explained that indeed, if you buy and sell real estate too often, CRA may disallow your claim for the principal residence exemption. Even worse, they could disallow the capital gains treatment usually used on the sale of real estate and other assets.

"Recall that this capital gains treatment comes with a 50% inclusion rate. But, CRA could require the reporting of 100% of the gain as a gross profit if they think you are in the business of buying and selling homes," he said. "The more closely your business or occupation is related to commercial real estate transactions, for example, if you are a real estate broker or builder, the more likely it is that any gain realized from such a transaction will not qualify for the principal residence exemption at all and be considered business income rather than a capital gain."

"Wow, that's good to know. I do a lot of real estate transactions in my law firm," Chet noted.

"The courts have considered some of the following criteria on a case-by-case basis to guide us in assessing the right tax filing requirements," Malcolm told him. He then proceed to write some of the criteria on the white board:

- taxpayer's intention for the property at the time of its purchase,
- feasibility of the plans,
- geographical location and zoned use of the real estate acquired,
- any evidence that intentions changed after purchase of the property,
- the nature of the business, profession, calling or trade of the taxpayer and his/her associates,
- the extent to which borrowed money was used to finance the acquisition and the terms of the financing,
- the length of time the property was held by the taxpayer,
- factors which motivated the sale of the real estate, and
- evidence that the taxpayer and/or his/her associates had dealt extensively in real estate.

"It's good to keep notes of your circumstances in anticipation of meeting the criteria," Malcolm advised. "Once we meet with an auditor, if ever, they would come in handy."

"There's one more concept I'd like you know before you go today, Chet," Malcolm knew the young father had to get home for dinner. "If your employer requires you to move at least 40 kilometres closer to your place of employment, you may wish to keep your principal residence and rent it out while you are gone. In that case, it is possible to elect no change in use and designate that property as your principal residence while you are gone. "

"That's another interesting tax factoid, Malcolm!" Chet was again amused by his accountant's vast and profound knowledge of all these little tax facts. They had saved them many dollars over the years. "For the election to be valid, you must move back into the home before the end of the year in which your employment terminates, however."

"We'll chat about moving expenses related to the home if that ever happens. For example," Malcolm was on a roll, "Where the move is required by the employer and you sell your home at a loss, it is possible to receive a tax free reimbursement of those losses, in amounts up to $15,000, should your employer choose to assist you."

"Very cool," Chet smiled as he reached for his overcoat. It had begun to snow in the meantime.

"What would happen if I couldn't sell my home before leaving," Chet peered fearfully out at the howling wind. "And really, I would say yes if someone wanted to offer me a stint in Jamaica right now!"

Malcolm started opening the door to what seemed to be a mini-blizzard. "Try to remember this: you could claim up to $5,000 as a moving expense for the costs at the old residence, including mortgage interest, property taxes, insurance and utilities."

"You rock, Malcolm," Chet scurried out, his head tucked as far into his collar as possible.

The Money Moral

Your principal residence can be a great investment if you can use the principal residence exemption to your advantage. But, if you flip your principal residences often enough, the gains may be fully included in income. Therefore guard your access to the exemption well; it can significantly increase your net worth, but you do need to know the tax filing rules.

Quickie Tax Quiz

1. How many tax-exempt principal residences can a family have?

2. If you have more than one home that qualifies as a principal residence, when do you have to decide which will be designated as your principal residence?

3. Why is claiming CCA on your home office a bad idea?

   Check out the answers in *Family Tax Essentials Portal* at www.knowledgebureau.com.

FIRST RENTAL
PROPERTIES

Thomas and Beverley delighted in their travels. They had found a lovely condo in the south and tried to get down for a couple of weeks right after Christmas, and in really cold years, in March, too. This year, with that third grandchild, however, they put up their place on an internet rental site. A great young couple would be taking their place and paying them rent, too.

It was a great way to save up some airline ticket money and in fact, Thomas was surprised how much people were willing to pay to stay in their condo. He was receiving $5,000 US per month and definitely had the possibility of renting it out for the winter months, if he wanted to.

Malcolm was called in to consult on reporting the rental income. "That's wonderful news all around – new baby and new income sources! How is Catherine feeling?" Malcolm was really fond of the young family, and almost as proud as Thomas and Beverley. They were all delighted that the pregnancy was completely uneventful so far.

"Income and expenses will be reported on a calendar year basis, and it would be a good idea to start a separate bank account for the rental income, which will have to be reported in equivalent Canadian dollars on your returns."

Malcolm counselled his clients in making sure that the condo is valued now that it will have a rental use. He explained that the value would have to be reported on a *Foreign Income Verification Statement* as well, if over $100,000, and if the property is used as a rental more than 50% of the time. In addition, Malcolm shared that a withholding tax on rental income would be required to be paid in the U.S., and this could be recovered by filing a 1040NR *U.S. Non Resident Alien Income Tax Return*.

"In addition, you may not be able to write off losses if you can't justify that you are charging rent at fair market value. Take newspaper clippings, online rental value scans, and other proof of rentals in the area for us to add to your permanent records so you can make a case for what you are charging, especially if you ever rent to a related person."

Malcolm also explained that any advance payments of rent can be included in income according to the years they relate to. Lease cancellation payments received are also included in rental income.

"What's deductible from that rental income, Malcolm?" Beverley wanted to be sure their recordkeeping would be up to speed.

"First, I need to tell you that to deduct operating expenses from rental income, there must be a reasonable expectation of profit on an annual basis. Fully deductible operating expenses include maintenance, repairs, supplies, interest, and taxes."

Malcolm rose to write on his white board:

Trap #1 Maintenance and repairs are 100% deductible, he explained but improvements over the original condition or that extend the useful life of the asset are added to the cost base of the condo. "I would record these expenses on the Capital Cost Allowance (CCA) statements instead. But once again, we likely wouldn't claim CCA if you're planning on choosing the condo as your tax exempt principal residence."

"It's unlikely Malcolm," Thomas said, "but a good point."

Trap #2 Don't deduct any personal living expenses.

Trap #3 Family member rentals may be exempt. "If you are renting a room in your home to your nephew, Charlie, for the cost of the groceries, there is no expectation of profit, and you would not be able to deduct a rental loss against other income," Malcolm warned. "But in this case, unless there is a demonstrable profit motive, you wouldn't need to report the income, either."

"Aside from that," Malcolm said, "there were a number of common deductible operating expenses to keep receipts for, my friends." He then sent Thomas and Beverley off with a checklist:

- **Advertising costs**
- **Condominium Fees:** Applicable to the period when the rental condo was available for rent.
- **Insurance:** If the insurance is prepaid for future years, claim only the portion that applies to the rental year.
- **Landscaping:** We would deduct this in the year paid.
- **Legal Fees:** If they are incurred to prepare leases or to collect rent, they are deductible. But if they are incurred to acquire the property, they are added to its cost base. Finally, if they are paid on the sale of the property, they are considered to be outlays and expenses which will reduce any capital gain on the sale.
- **Accounting fees** to prepare statements, keep books, or prepare the tax return are deductible.
- **Maintenance and Repairs:** Costs of regular maintenance and minor repairs are deductible. For major repairs, it must be determined if the cost is a current expense (restoration) or capital in nature (improvement).
- **Management and Administration Fees:** If you pay a third party to manage or otherwise look after some aspect of the property, the amount paid is deductible.
- **Mortgage Interest:** Interest on a mortgage to purchase the property plus any interest on additional loans to improve the rental property may be deducted, provided you can show there is a reasonable expectation of profit from the revenue property. Note that if an additional mortgage is taken out against the equity in the property and the proceeds are used for some other purpose, the mortgage interest is not deductible as a rental expense, but may be deductible as a carrying charge if the proceeds were used to earn investment income. Other charges relating to the acquisition of a mortgage (banking fees, for example) are not deductible in the year paid, but can be amortized over a five-year period starting at the time they were incurred.

If the interest costs relate to the acquisition of depreciable property, you may elect to add the interest to the capital cost of the asset rather than deduct it in the year paid. This will be beneficial if, for example, the property generates a rental loss and you don't have enough other income to absorb the loss.

- **Office and Other Supplies:** Office and other supplies used up in earning rental income are deductible as are home office expenses in situations where you use the office to keep books or serve tenants. The rules for self-employment would apply to home office expense in this case.

- **Property Taxes:** These are deductible.

- **Renovations for the Disabled:** Costs incurred to make the rental property accessible to individuals with a mobility impairment may be fully deducted.

- **Utilities:** If costs are paid by the landlord and not reimbursed by the tenant, they will be deductible. Costs charged to tenants are deductible if amounts collected are included in rental income.

Malcolm reminded them again that on the Canadian tax return, world income must be reported in Canadian funds and therefore exchange rates must be used and calculated.

"Will there are tax consequences as a result?" Thomas asked.

Malcolm explained that indeed there could be, and that quarterly instalment payments could be affected, too. In addition, gains or losses resulting from foreign currency transactions themselves have tax consequences. "The tax outcomes are linked to the nature of the transactions – whether they follow an income account (from a business transaction) or as a result of a capital disposition."

He went on. "In general, tax filers must report currency gains in excess of $200 as capital gains; ignore amounts of capital gains or losses less than this. Foreign currency gains and losses must be reported at the exchange rate in effect on the day the currency was exchanged, but as long as filing methods are consistent, average exchange rate calculations may be allowed."

Thomas had another question. "Does this apply to travellers cheques purchased in a foreign currency for a trip abroad and then converted back to Canadian dollars upon landing back home?"

Malcolm replied that first, they would determine if the amounts were over the $200 threshold. "If so, any gains on the currency exchange above this will be reported as a capital gain; any losses will be reported as a capital loss."

"When might a loss happen?" Malcolm explained that those who acquired a foreign personal use property only to experience a foreign exchange loss on the repayment of a debt used to acquire the property, will be happy to know that those foreign currency losses can be claimed as a capital loss.

It was time to go. "In the meantime, as the two of you jointly own this property, each of you will show half the revenues, expenses and profits or losses on your return," Malcolm said as he helped his clients to the door. "I will worry about that, though!"

The Money Moral

Rental properties can increase wealth in two ways: by providing rental income to help pay for the mortgage and if values increase by increasing net worth. However, revenue properties are often audited, so be sure you stay out of the rental property compliance traps which trip up many taxpayers.

Quickie Tax Quiz

1. What is required in order to claim expenses of operating a rental?

2. If you collect $10,000 in rental income and have $8,000 in deductible rental expenses, how much rental income is taxed on your tax return?

3. If you collect $10,000US in rental income and have $8,000US in deductible rental expenses, how much rental income is taxed on your Canadian return?

   Check out the answers in *Family Tax Essentials Portal* at www.knowledgebureau.com.

HOW NON-REGISTERED
INVESTMENTS ARE TAXED

Chet and Malcolm were discussing his parents' new rental venture when they next met. Malcolm was relishing the opportunity to explain another section of the *Income Tax Act*, and this time the topic would be "income from property" held in non-registered accounts.

"When money is invested in a non-registered investment account or a rental property; it generates what's known as "income from property" and this can include interest, dividends, royalties or rents, as in your parents' case. Essentially this is passive, rather than actively earned income, and it's added to income annually when the personal tax return is filed."

He explained that any increase in value of the underlying income-producing assets is treated differently. "There is no tax accounting until there is a disposition; either an actual one which results in sales proceeds being received, or a 'deemed disposition', which can occur without the exchange of money, for example, on transfer of assets or the death of a taxpayer. This type of income – the increase in value over the original cost of the asset – is known as a capital gain, and as you well know, only 50% of gains are added to income."

Losses, of course, could occur as well. Chet remembered talking about tax loss harvesting as part of their year-end tax planning discussions with Malcolm.

Chet wanted to learn more about investing in non-registered accounts, as he had earned a bonus on his last assignment and had already topped up his TFSA and RRSP. Malcolm, as usual, came to the rescue as his financial educator in guiding his thoughts around investment options.

"Income from property held in a non-registered account will usually produce interest, dividends, or other passive income. Much of this is reported on T-slips: a T3 slip from investments held in a trust, a T5 slip when the source is a corporation, a T5013 slip from an investment in a limited partnership, or a T5008 slip for securities transactions. In some cases, this income will be self-reported."

But Malcolm went on to explain that an issue facing investors in recent times: very low rates of return some of their investments. "A $10,000 deposit earning half of one per cent, for example, will only have earned $50 for the year. Financial institutions, however, need only issue a slip if the earnings are $50 or more," he said. "So, investors must self-report interest on deposits under this. That's why I will always remind you to dig out your bank books or statements, as well as your Notice of Assessment or Reassessment to find any interest paid to you from CRA, which is reportable, too."

The two also reviewed the joint account reporting rules. Malcolm used a recent example from his class at the university to do so. Malcolm loved teaching taxes and had found another outlet to do so. The example went like this:

"Debra, who normally stays home and raises the children, deposited all of the money that she inherited from her father in a joint account with her husband. In this case, 100% of the earnings are reported by Debra," he said. "If her husband, Jason, who earns all the other income for the family, deposited 100% of savings in another joint account, he reports 100% of the earnings from that account. A third account holds their gain on the sale of their principal residence last year; to which they each contributed one half of the cash gifts they received from their wedding. In this case, each spouse reports 50% of the interest earnings."

Chet understood. He wanted to switch gears, however. "What about the dividends I hope to earn from these new investments?"

"As you know," Malcolm began, "dividends are earned as a result of an investment by an individual in a corporation, that is incorporated and resident in Canada. Dividends are the after-tax distribution of earnings by a company."

He explained that when dividend amounts are reported on the income tax return of the individual shareholder, the actual dividends received are "grossed up" so the taxpayer reports an amount higher than that received.

"Offsetting this grossed-up amount is a 'Dividend Tax Credit' (DTC), which is computed on Schedule 1, the *Detailed Tax Calculation*. This credit reduces federal taxes payable. A provincial credit is also calculated. The objective with these calculations is to integrate the corporate and personal tax systems to avoid double taxation. The income is grossed up so the investor reports the amount that the corporation had to earn in order to pay the dividend. Then the dividend tax credit reduces the investor's taxes by the amount of taxes the corporation paid on the income earned to pay the dividend. The end result is a lower marginal tax rate on the dividend income reported personally."

Malcolm explained that the amount of the gross-up and DTC will depend on the size of the company because larger companies pay taxes at higher rates and so the gross up and DTC are higher. He also explained that the increased gross-up may be problematic for taxpayers who are in a clawback zone for non-refundable tax credits, refundable tax credits, or the OAS or EI Benefits. "This may, in fact, reduce or eliminate these provisions, and we will want to plan your investment income sources with this in mind," he said. "An RRSP contribution will also reduce net income to protect your family's benefits, Chet."

Malcolm provided another example of tax efficiency for lower earners; just in case Catherine's income dropped this year. "Where income is in the lowest tax bracket, the dividend tax credit may a "negative marginal tax rate". What this means is that the dividend tax credit will help to offset taxes owing on other types of income earned in the year, and that makes dividends in low tax brackets very tax efficient."

In addition, there was an interesting exception to the Attribution Rules, which generally require the spouse who earned and invested the capital that generated the dividends be the one to report the dividend income. "If the lower-income spouse has dividends, but cannot benefit from the dividend tax credit because his or her income is too low, the higher-income spouse may report the dividends. But only if a spousal amount is created or increased by removing the dividends from the lower-income spouse's income."

Chet's eyes were starting to glaze over. Usually he loved this stuff, but the twins had been under the weather and neither of their parents had had much sleep. Yet he knew he did need to hear about the potential for Alternative Minimum Taxes or AMT as Malcolm called it. He poured himself a cup of coffee as Malcolm spoke.

"Taxpayers who receive a large part of their income by way of eligible dividends may find themselves subject to Alternative Minimum Tax. This will happen if the dividend tax credit entirely eliminates tax otherwise payable. This calculation is complicated and I won't take the time to explain it to you today," Chet was grateful; then he noticed the mirth in his tax mentor's eyes.

"Just remember this, if you ever have to pay minimum tax, we'll be able to offset regular taxes payable in the following seven years until the minimum tax balance is used up. But if you continue to earn a large part of your income from dividends, you may continue to be subject to minimum tax which you may never be able to recover."

Chet wanted to understand what "Capital Gains Dividends" were. He was tired, but felt he really should know more, especially as investment strategies seemed to erupt constantly as a favorite subject in the office. "These dividends are received from mutual fund companies and reported on a T5 slip. They reflect capital gains realized in the fund rather than on disposition of the investment. These 'dividends' are eligible for a 50% income inclusion."

"What about these dividend reinvestment plans I have been hearing so much about," Chet asked?

Malcolm was happy to provide him with his response: "When a corporation reinvests the dividends they should distribute to you, to buy additional shares of the corporation instead, the amount of the dividend is included in income in the tax year the cash dividend would have ordinarily been paid. The cost base of the asset is then increased by the amount of the reinvestment. This is a popular method used by mutual funds and segregated funds."

Chet also wanted to know how foreign dividends are handled. "Foreign dividends do not qualify for the gross up and dividend tax credit that Canadian dividends do. Rather, the actual amounts are reported in Canadian funds when received. If the dividends were subject to withholding taxes in the foreign country, we will claim a foreign tax credit federally and often provincially too."

The rules are complicated, of course, and Malcolm explained that the amount of withholding tax is determined by the tax treaty in force between Canada and the foreign country. "In general, though, the withholding tax rate is 15% for non-residents of countries with whom we have a tax treaty, and 25% for those resident in non-treaty countries."

He also took the time to let Chet know about new reporting rules for assets held offshore. "Canadian residents holding investments in U.S. securities may have tax consequences in both countries; dividends earned on U.S. securities, for example, are taxed in the U.S. first through withholding taxes and then in Canada, subject to the foreign tax credit rules we discussed earlier. Portfolio gains on U.S. securities held by Canadians will be taxed in Canada."

He then explained the potential need to complete Form T1135 *Foreign Income Verification Statement*. "This is required if your 'specified' foreign properties have a cumulative cost of $100,000 or more, although simplified reporting will be allowed if the values are under $250,000."

The taxation of interest income was covered next; although there was not much to report by taxpayers with the recent low rates. Chet knew of many interest-bearing investments: Guaranteed Investment Certificates (GICs), Canada Savings Bonds (CSBs), Treasury Bills or T-Bills, strip bonds or income bonds, or debentures, which link interest paid to a corporation's profits or cash flow. Indexed debt obligations can be linked to inflation, too.

He wanted Chet to pay particular attention to a tax trap that was unavoidable when interest income was earned in a compounding investments. "An investment compounds when earnings are reinvested so that you can earn interest on those earnings as well as the principal. But for compounding investments annual reporting is required."

Chet was surprised to learn this. "Yes, that's right, all interest that accrues in the year ending on the anniversary date must be reported, even though you will not yet have received the money, Chet."

"That makes the receipt of compounding interest very inefficient for tax purposes, especially at current low, low rates... taxes and inflation eat up the returns very quickly." Malcolm agreed.

"This is enough for today, though, Chet," Malcolm shooed his exhausted client out the door. "Besides, it's time for my saxophone lesson!" Chet was incredulous – the man continuously amazed him with his energy, wit and joie de vivre! Malcolm truly seemed to be living his Wealth Purpose.

The Money Moral

Earning dividend income can vastly improve marginal tax rates on investments held outside of a registered account. Dividends are much more tax efficient than interest. But they can also increase clawbacks of certain social benefits and credits. In addition, foreign dividends could attract additional filings, and expensive penalties if the reporting is delinquent. Tax advice is always important when investment strategies are planned with dividend income.

Quickie Tax Quiz

1. Which is more tax efficient: interest income or Canadian dividend income?

2. Why might dividends be less efficient if the taxpayer is in a clawback zone?

3. Under what circumstances do you have to report your foreign holdings on T1135 *Foreign Income Verification Statement?*

Check out the answers in **Family Tax Essentials Portal** at www.knowledgebureau.com.

REPORTING
GAINS AND
LOSSES

Chet was over-the-moon excited. His fists pumped the air above him and as he vaulted into his home he shouted Catherine's name. He couldn't wait to tell his very pregnant wife that he had just had a huge win on the stock market: the shares he purchased for $10 had doubled to $20. He had $50,000 in the bank; it was just like winning the lottery!

Catherine was absolutely thrilled. She felt like jumping up in down too, but restrained herself. She certainly didn't want to go into premature labour again. There was so much they could do with the money. Thomas would know how to plan this properly, but Catherine definitely was dreaming about a few luxuries, too.

When they got together with Chet's parents later that evening to celebrate, Catherine had some very basic questions. Just how would a capital gain be reported and calculated? How much of that $50,000 was really theirs to spend? Her father-in-law explained that a capital gain is based on the following equation:

Proceeds of Disposition – Adjusted Cost Base – Outlays and Expenses = Capital Gain (or Loss),

"One half of this capital gain is included in your taxable income, Catherine. The income inclusion rate, in other words, is 50%. The costs of disposing of a capital property may be used to reduce a capital gain or increase a loss, as the case may be. This might include advertising costs, brokerage fees, commissions, costs incurred to improve the property, finder's fees, professional fees: legal, surveyor's, appraisals, and transfer taxes."

"Capital losses are important, too," Chet added. "They can reduce or eliminate capital gains of the current year, the prior three years or any future year."

Dinner continued with discussions about the twins' latest antics, and the happy growth of the family. Catherine and her mother-in-law giggled about the new budget for decorating, spas and vacations! The tax talk was shelved for the evening and not picked up again until the next meeting with Malcolm was scheduled.

Catherine settled in for a longer explanation as her baby kicked gently at her tummy. Chet's hand on her tummy was always so reassuring. Malcolm began to explain the various categories of capital properties for tax purposes, trying to keep things light, despite the complicated rules.

"Let's start with what's known as 'personal-use properties'. The gains and losses on the sale of a personal-use property, such as homes, cars, boats and furniture, must be reported on the tax return, but these assets are subject to what's known as the '$1,000 Rule.' In my world that simply means that the Proceeds of Disposition and Adjusted Cost Base of your personal-use property are deemed to be no less than $1,000 for the purposes of computing any gain or loss. This eliminates reporting small transactions. But what's important for you to know is that losses on personal-use properties are not deductible. You take those personally." He then embellished:

"Peter put a lot of money into his cabin at the lake. He bought it for $50,000 and then put in a deck and an addition for another $50,000. He did not use it as a rental property and after a year, he had to sell it for only $80,000 as he took a job in another city. His $20,000 loss, unfortunately, is not deductible."

"What about the coin collection my grandfather left me, Malcolm? Is that reportable when I sell it?" Catherine hoped there was an incredible treasure inside that old box.

"Well Catherine, these types of possessions, called listed personal property, usually don't depreciate in value. They can include artwork, jewelry, rare books or stamp collections, too. Again the $1,000 Rule applies, however, in this case, losses can be deducted but only against other listed personal property gains of the year. If there are none, you can apply unabsorbed losses by carrying them back three years or forward seven years but only against gains on listed personal property."

Chet wanted to know more about the reporting of capital dispositions for three types of assets: publicly traded shares, mutual fund units, other shares he was investing in; bonds, debentures and promissory notes; and a piece of vacant land he had his eye on.

"Let's start with the securities," Malcolm suggested.

He explained that for many tax filers, the reporting of capital transactions for mutual or segregated funds is really easy. "We simply enter the amounts from the T-slips and the tax software will keep track of any unabsorbed capital losses as well. These transactions reflect trading within managed accounts and the resulting capital gains and other income that has flowed through to the investor."

However, Malcolm went on to explain that when the securities or mutual fund units themselves are sold or disposed of, that disposition is reported separately. "For these reasons, we keep meticulous records of the cost of acquisition and any additions (reinvested amounts in the case of mutual or segregated funds) as well as outlays and expenses (such as brokerage fees) to properly compute the Adjusted Cost Base (ACB). This can be tricky in some cases, but I'm on top of it."

Chet and Catherine were so grateful for that. "I understand that shares in the same class of the same corporation or units in a specific mutual fund are known as 'identical properties'. How are they different?"

"Yes," said Malcolm. "Each share or unit is the same as the others in this case, and you can't tell one from another. When you trade a portion of a group of identical properties, the average cost of all properties in the group must be calculated to determine the adjusted cost base (ACB) of the property sold in order to report the capital gain or loss. Simply stated, each time there is a purchase, we add the adjusted cost base of all the shares or mutual units in the group and divide by the total number of shares or units held."

Catherine had curled herself into a ball next to Chet. She was sound asleep. The men smiled at her peacefulness – things would soon ramp up and Catherine deserved the extra rest. They carried on with an example of an identical shares transaction.

Malcom started with an example. "Suppose that on January 1,

Sarah purchased 1,000 shares of QRS Corp. for $12,000. On March 15, she purchased another 1,000 shares in the same corporation for $8,000. Then she disposes of 1,000 shares on July 15, for $11,000. There are no other transactions in the year and for these purposes, no outlays or expenses. The capital gain to be reported is calculated as follows." The calculation was assembled:

- The average cost of the share is: ($12,000 + $8,000) / 2,000 = $10 per share.
- The Adjusted Cost Base of the shares she sold is $10/share x 1,000 shares or $10,000.
- The Capital Gain is $11,000 – $10,000 or $1,000.
- This is reported on Schedule 3.
- Half of this is added to total income.

"Chet, you should also know that in the year you acquire a mutual fund, you will usually receive a full annual distribution, even if you invested late in the year. This might be an unpleasant surprise at tax time. These amounts will generally be reinvested for you and you'll need to keep track of this to increase your cost base."

"Got it," Chet had another important question, however. "What if I exchange an investment in one fund for another, like switching from an equity fund into a balanced fund?"

"Well in that case, a taxable disposition is considered to have occurred, Chet. However, there are no tax consequences if the investment is in corporate class funds." Malcolm then went into a longer explanation about this asset.

"Corporate class funds," he explained, "are mutual fund corporations with multiple share classes – each of which constitutes a different fund. The primary advantage is that investors can switch between mutual funds within the same corporation without triggering a capital gain. In addition, because all expenses and non-capital losses are allocated against income across all share classes within the corporate structure, taxable distributions can be reduced. Because those taxable distributions are paid as eligible dividends or capital gains dividends, they are taxed more advantageously than ordinary income or interest would be within a non-registered account."

"Reporting for corporate class funds differs from other mutual funds, as well. Any distributions or allocations are reported at tax time on a

T5 slip rather than a T3 Slip. T-series corporate class funds can offer a regular tax efficient income stream by blending a return of capital with distributions. After you've removed your principal," Malcolm explained, "there will be future capital gains tax consequences because the adjusted cost base has changed. However, at that time the investor may be able to offset capital gains with losses of the current or prior years."

"We can't complete this discussion, Chet, without mentioning segregated funds." Malcolm explained that these are mutual funds wrapped up with a life insurance policy to provide a death benefit as well as a guarantee of principal. "The money is held in trust and income is distributed to the beneficiaries and then generally immediately reinvested, much like mutual fund distributions. Income allocations do not affect the value of the segregated fund, unlike mutual funds. In addition, capital losses can be flowed through to the segregated fund holder to offset other capital gains."

He explained that insurance segregated funds differ from mutual funds primarily in that they offer maturity and death guarantees on the capital invested and specifically, reset guarantees – the ability to lock in market gains. Depending on the insurer, a reset can be initiated by the investor two to four times per year. The guaranteed period on maturity is usually 10 years after the policy is purchased, or after the reset. There are no tax consequences at the time the accrued gains in the investment are locked in by way of reset. If the value of the fund has increased over the reset amount, the disposition is reported as a normal capital gain.

"I will have to get Catherine home soon, Malcolm, but let's discuss this vacant land transaction," said Chet, gingerly moving his wife to a more comfortable position.

Special rules apply to vacant land, Malcolm explained. "If it's held for speculation; that is there is no potential for income from the property, a capital gain or loss will eventually occur. Interest and property taxes cannot be deducted along the way, either, and you must be able to show the potential for rental income to deduct interest and property taxes. Unfortunately, if there is no potential for income, the expenses cannot be deducted."

There was a silver lining to this prohibitive tax treatment. "So long as the land is not held for personal use," Malcolm said, "interest and property taxes may be added to the adjusted cost base of the land to reduce the capital gain on disposition."

"What if I want to divide the land into lots and sell them off?" Chet was hoping the opportunity would prove lucrative in the future. "Vacant land that is capital property used by its owner for the purpose of gaining or producing income from the sale of lots will be treated as business assets," Malcolm offered. He then went on to explain that the lots will become inventory of the business and any profits will be taxed as business income. The lots will be considered to have been converted to inventory at the earlier of:

- the time when the owner starts making improvements with a view to selling it; and
- the time of making application for approval of a plan to subdivide the land into lots for sale, in order to develop a subdivision.

The subdivision of farmland or inherited land in order to sell it will not constitute a conversion to inventory and so capital gains treatment should be preserved in these cases.

"The buying and selling of assets can help you build your family's wealth significantly, Chet. You're on the right track in exploring the opportunities. Let's chat next time about controlling the timing of those transactions for the best tax consequences," Malcolm cautioned.

The Money Moral

Investments in assets outside of registered accounts can provide a variety of income sources that may or may not be tax efficient for the taxpayer. However, the tax deferred accrual of value in the underlying assets provides a great opportunity to build wealth while being well paid by the income generated.

Quickie Tax Quiz

1. What special rules apply to "personal-use property"?

2. What is "listed personal property" and how is it different from other personal-use property?

3. What are "identical properties"?

   Check out the answers in *Family Tax Essentials Portal* at www.knowledgebureau.com.

MANAGING THE COSTS OF INVESTING:
DEBT AND FEES

Building a Wealth Purpose with a Tax Strategy provides the fastest route to a worry-free financial future. Besides taxes, however, the costs of debt and professional fees can provide a significant drag and, in fact, a risk that must be managed.

Malcolm's opening lecture at his university class was being closely attended to by his 20 undergraduate students. They found financial education fascinating, as they all were in business school, hoping to help others with their finances in the future.

"It's hard to believe that back in 1980, Canadians' debt to disposable income level was 66%; today it is 164%, which means that households today owe more than $1.64 for every dollar of disposable income. That's a big problem if job loss is in the future. Astute financial advisors will want to be sure this is a topic of conversation before any debt is taken on, and especially for those working in industries suffering downturns, or as part of any retirement planning conversations." The students took careful note.

Malcolm threw out a relevant example. "Think of your student loans for a moment. It's a big process to receive one and usually there is much resourcing when that happens. But, one of the underlying conditions of borrowing of any kind is simple: there must be a strategy for paying back both the principal and the interest. How many of you would agree that there is not enough counsel on paying back a student loan at the time it is provided to you?" Numerous hands rose in the air. He reminded them that student loan interest could be claimed as a non-refundable tax credit on the personal return when it's paid.

"People with multiple types of debt must also prioritize which should be paid first," Malcolm said. "What should be paid first if you have a student loan, a mortgage and an investment loan? What if you owe money to the Canada Revenue Agency? And how about that credit card debt?" He could see that there were a few cringes and eyes that rolled upwards. It pained him to see that debt was already a part of these young peoples' lives.

He explained that, after credit cards, one of the most expensive forms of debt is money owed to the tax department. CRA will charge the prescribed rate of interest, plus 4% more on the taxes owed. But they will also charge the same rate of interest on unpaid penalties such as penalties for late filing, gross negligence penalties and tax evasion, all of which can multiply the cost of the original tax debt many, many times over.

CRA can also require employers to send portions of employee's income by garnisheeing wages; the same is true of pensions. "Not only can they shut down your income, but they can take away your assets," he said. There were a few gasps in the room at that point. "Therefore tax debt requires immediate attention and should be paid first."

The lesson went on. "Non-deductible debt should be tackled next. This includes expensive credit card debt and the debt attached to buying a personal residence. Interest costs here are not deductible. Neither is interest paid when money is borrowed to invest in a registered savings plan like an RRSP or TFSA. You need to make note of this in your planning,"

Malcolm faced the class at this point. "It may, however, still be to your benefit to borrow to invest in an RRSP despite the fact that you can't deduct your interest costs. Why would that be smart?"

Several students in the room looked completely blank; but others remembered the tax estimations they had worked on, and the expensive clawbacks of Canada Child Benefits families are subject to as income rises. "An RRSP would reduce net income and therefore high marginal tax rates in those instances," a young mother in the class responded.

The lesson then moved on to the topic of deductible debt. "This includes interest you paid on money borrowed for non-registered investments," Malcolm began, "but, the onus of proof is on you to establish that the borrowed funds are being used for the purposes of earning income from a business, or from investment assets or from your rental property."

When money is borrowed to buy securities, on the other hand, the investment must have the potential to produce "income from property." Malcolm explained that if the investment does not carry a stated interest or dividend rate, which might be the case with some common shares or mutual funds, the interest costs on an investment loan may not be deductible. "CRA will generally allow interest costs on funds borrowed to buy common shares to be deductible if there is a possibility of receiving dividends, whether or not they are actually received, but each case may be assessed individually upon audit," he stated.

"What happens if I borrowed big on my margin account with my investment advisor, to invest in something like Nortel, only to lose most of my money? Can I still deduct the interest on the outstanding loan?" Malcolm's student Jason was the son of a portfolio manager and knew well the stories of success and failure in the financial markets.

"If the source of income for which you borrowed no longer exists or has substantially diminished, you may indeed continue to write off the interest on the loan as if the underlying asset still existed," said Malcolm. "The amount considered 'not to be lost' must however be traceable to the loan you are paying off. And, if you dispose of the asset at a loss, you may continue to write off the interest costs so long as the proceeds were used to pay down the loan amount."

The discussion next turned to the repayment of the various debts themselves. "It can pay handsome dividends to borrow for the right things: to get an education, to purchase income-producing financial assets, rental properties and homes in which tax exempt gains accrue," Malcolm began. "However, a 'Plan B' must be readily available if the source of funding that debt disappears in order to contain your costs and minimize your stress."

He asked his class what buckets of money they would tap into to pay down debt. Taking money out of a TFSA seemed like a good plan to some of the students and Malcolm concurred. "There are no tax consequences, which is good, and the money withdrawn can be recontributed to the TFSA without penalty, providing reinvestment guidelines are met."

"Another alternative is repayment from other tax-paid capital that is earning a lower return than the interest costs," offered another student. He cited the examples of a term deposit, or a Canada Savings Bond.

Yet another student suggested that the tax refund or other social benefits that are not yet allocated to another purpose be used to pay down debt.

Malcolm agreed that these were all good solutions. "Least attractive options include any withdrawal that generates taxes: money taken out of an RRSP, for example, or disposition of a capital asset with a large accrued gain," he said. He then added another couple of tax factoids:

He told the class that if they borrowed against the cash value in a life insurance policy to then invest the money in the stock market, it was possible to claim the interest paid as a carrying charge. "But, if the interest is not repaid but rather deducted from the value of the insurance, you'll need to complete *Form T2210 Verification of Life Insurance Policy Loan Interest*, when you file your tax return."

Malcolm then looked at the time and changed course. "I want to finish this lesson on a different note today." He seemed unusually solemn and this brought a silent and focused attention from the students in the class.

"Wealth will be eroded by taxes and debt, but also by the fees charged by financial services firms and advisors. It's important to minimize these costs and if they are necessary, to make sure they are deductible. Fees charged in the financial services industry can vary with the type of investment and so product selection is important."

Malcolm put an example on the white board. It was a $10,000 investment in an RRSP each year for 25 years earning an average 8% return. "This investment will grow to over $700,000," he said. "However, a 2% management fee attached to this may represent as much as 25% of the total gain this investment will earn. That is 2% in fees is 25% of an 8% return. When we extrapolate this forward, the fees payable would in fact erode away over $182,000 out of the growth of this investment."

The students were incredulous. None of them had ever thought this figure could be so large.

Malcolm reminded them that the cost of investing in bonds, GICs or other interest-producing assets can also be expensive. "The management fee is the spread between what an institution will pay on its debt instruments vs. what it will charge its customers to borrow money. Think about that, and then add the rate of taxation and inflation to discover the rate of return you require to break even." Even the mathematically challenged in the audience knew it was much more than the paltry sums being delivered today.

"Being able to deduct some of these costs will preserve your wealth, but the rules are specific," Malcolm continued. "Fees paid to a financial, investment or wealth advisor or advisory firm, other than commissions, are deductible on the tax return if they are paid for advice on buying or selling securities or for the administration of those assets."

However what he said next surprised the class: "Fees paid to stockbrokers are not deductible unless the broker also provides investment portfolio management and administration services for which a separate fee is charged. Also not deductible are fees paid for newspaper, newsletter or magazine subscriptions or fees paid to a trustee of an RRSP or TFSA."

The Money Moral

Debt can erode wealth if not managed. If you are going to borrow money, prepare a deliberate strategy for repayment of debt in a timely cost-effective order. Interest costs as well as professional fees may be tax deductible but this will depend on whether they are incurred to earn income from property or to acquire capital. The costs must be traceable to investment purposes. Always stay clear of tax debt.

Quickie Tax Quiz

1. If your debts include a home mortgage, student loan, car loan and CRA balance, which should you work at paying off first?

2. Under what circumstances might it make sense to borrow to make an RRSP contribution even though you can't deduct the interest you pay?

3. Why are fees charged on investments important to wealth growth?

Check out the answers in *Family Tax Essentials Portal* at www.knowledgebureau.com.

THE MONEY MORALS:
GROW and MANAGE
MONEY BUCKETS

Prioritize Your Money Buckets. The tax homes you find for the dollars you earn will diversify your income sources, thereby averaging down the taxes you pay. That provides an interesting embellishment to your Personal and Family Net Worth Statements: an order in which to make your investments. So what comes first – the RRSP or the TFSA? It's going to depend on your age, your income sources and your commitment to your Wealth Potential.

Take Advantage of Your Principal Residence Exemption. Your principal residence can be a great investment if you can use the principal residence exemption to your advantage. But, if you flip your principal residences often enough, the gains may be fully included in income. Therefore guard your access to the exemption well; it can significantly increase your net worth, but you do need to know the tax filing rules.

Build on Your Real Estate. Rental properties can increase wealth in two ways: by providing rental income to help pay for the mortgage and, if values increase, by increasing net worth. However, revenue properties are often audited, so be sure you stay out of the rental property compliance traps which trip up many taxpayers.

Diversify with Dividend Income. Earning dividend income can vastly improve marginal tax rates on investment held outside of a registered account. Dividends are much more tax efficient than interest. But they can also increase clawbacks of certain social benefits and credits. In addition, foreign dividends could attract additional filings, and expensive penalties if the reporting is delinquent. Tax advice is always important when investment strategies are planned with dividend income.

Grow Value in Capital Assets Without Paying Tax. Investments in assets outside of registered accounts can provide a variety of income sources that may or may not be tax efficient for the taxpayer. However, the tax deferred accrual of value in the underlying assets provides a great opportunity to build wealth while being well paid by the income generated.

Manage the Cost of Acquiring Assets. Debt can erode wealth if not managed. If you are going to borrow money, prepare a deliberate strategy for repayment of debt in a timely cost-effective order. Interest costs as well as professional fees may be tax deductible but this will depend on whether they are incurred to earn income from property or to acquire capital. The costs must be traceable to investment purposes. Always stay clear of tax debt.

PROCESS CHART – The following chart summarizes how invested capital and resulting income grows. Column 2 identifies whether money is invested with whole dollars, before taxes, or after taxes are paid. How many of these "money buckets" have you started? What is the Wealth Purpose for each?

Investment Option	Before- or After-Tax Dollars	Taxation of Income Earned	Taxation on Disposition or Withdrawal
Pensions			
RRSP / RPP	Before-Tax	Tax Deferred until withdrawal	Income & Principal Fully Taxable
RDSP*	After-Tax	"	Income Fully Taxable
CPP	Before-Tax	"	"
OAS	Non-contributory	n/a	"
Financial Assets			
TFSA	After-Tax	Tax Exempt	Non-Taxable
RESP	After-Tax	Tax Deferred	Income is Fully Taxable
Life Insurance	After-Tax	Tax Sheltered	Non-Taxable Death Benefit
Non-Registered Account	After-Tax	Depends on income source**	Tax on growth in value of Income-producing assets
Non-Financial Assets			
Principal Residence	After-Tax	Net Rental Income is Taxed Annually	Tax Exempt
Rental Property	After-Tax	"	Taxed On Growth in Value
Vacation Property	After-Tax	"	"

*Registered Disability Savings Plan

**interest, dividends, capital gains, business income, etc.

PART 6 – PRESERVE

EXCEEDING THE MEAN:
PROTECT YOUR LIFESTYLE

You have learned that having a Wealth Purpose is necessary if you are going to be successful in accumulating the assets you need to provide for your future income or *lifestyle.*

The objective is to invest as much of today's income as possible, grow it with diversified investment choices and then preserve it, fighting off wealth eroders along the way. We have discussed big ones already: taxes, debt, and professional fees. Another one is inflation.

The Bank of Canada defines inflation to be "a persistent rise in the cost of living." [1] The Consumer Price Index (CPI) measures that cost of living. Over the past several years, the Bank of Canada tried to keep inflation at around 2 per cent.

When rates of return on your investments exceed the CPI, your invested dollars remain "whole." Optimal rates of return should also provide a gain over taxation and fees paid.

While inflation robs your money of its purchasing power over time, it does favors for the Taxman. A common example is called "bracket creep". It works like this: in some provinces, tax brackets are not fully indexed to reflect the rate of inflation. Meanwhile, incomes tend to grow with the rate of inflation. As a result, your income is pushed into a higher tax bracket, and you pay tax at a higher rate.

The value of your tax credits can be similarly reduced when income-tested ceilings are not indexed to inflation. The result is that your income is pushed into a "clawback zone" sooner, thereby cutting into the size of your refundable and non-refundable credits.

---

[1] Statistics Canada, The Daily, April 17, 2014

You'll also get a smaller tax benefit from non-refundable tax credits when certain maximum threshold limits fail to be indexed to inflation; for example the $2,000 pension income amount, or the $5,000 maximum tuition, education and textbook transfer.

Investors are affected in other ways, too. When savers delay making their RRSP contributions, they not only miss out on the immediate tax reductions and the significant income deferral of today's "whole dollars," but they face a gap in potential tax sheltering. That's because inflation erodes away the value of the unused RRSP contribution room.

But one of the most expensive taxation results for asset-rich investors is this: capital assets can be over-valued due to increases in inflation. The Taxman wins in a big way in those cases, by taxing inflated values on the disposition of the assets. This also happens because the adjusted cost base, upon which capital gains are calculated in the first place, is not indexed to inflation.

So what can you do to hedge against inflation and protect your assets, to secure full purchasing power for today's dollars in the future? First, make sure you earn more money, year over year, than the rate of inflation. That's easier for younger people to do, but those who are retired must make sure rates of return they receive from the work of their accumulated assets will beat inflation rates. Stocks typically tend to do so; however, they come with market volatility. It's been tougher to stay ahead of inflation when holdings consist primarily of debt instruments. Reducing investment costs will help.

Real estate is a good hedge against inflation, because the value of real estate rises in inflationary times. Some seniors may wish to rethink their downsizing dreams and hold on to their tax exempt principal residences for these reasons.

While the rate of inflation is largely out of the control of investors, it can be mitigated with a sound Tax Strategy. The objective is to increase cash flow in the short term and protect asset values from taxation over the long run. Here are five things you can do to hedge against inflation with your Tax Strategy:

- Monitor net income levels of all family members carefully to make sure they are not exposed to clawback zones. If they are close to one, consider an RRSP contribution, if eligible.

- Split family income to stay out of the next tax bracket. This can be done through pension income splitting for those with eligible pension income, for example.
- Time the dispositions of your capital assets. You might decide, for example, to sell one half of your duplex in the current tax year and one half in the next to keep income levels in lower tax brackets in both years.
- Increase tax refunds by maximizing deductions and credits; then invest in a TFSA to avoid taxes completely.
- In inflationary times, rethink debt management. When the value of your rental property, for example, rises faster than interest rates, the value of your debt actually decreases. It may make sense to pay off this deductible debt over a longer time horizon; non-deductible debt sooner.

The Money Moral

It's most important to play defensively to beat inflation in building sustainable family wealth. Paying closer attention to rates of return and the costs of debt is critical; so is reducing the cost of fees and taxation. Your future lifestyle will depend on it.

BECOMING THE OUTLIER FAMILY:

PRINCIPLES FOR OUTSTANDING FINANCIAL SUCCESS

Chet and Catherine found that their Wealth Purpose changed as they moved in their lifecycle from singlehood, to marriage and parenthood. In addition, like most other people, they experienced financial events and economic events that would cause them to revisit their *Family Wealth Purpose* and measure it against short and long term needs and wants of their multiple generations.

Ultimately, what made them successful in their financial life was that they had a definitive approach to their money matters, backed up by a deliberate process for financial success. Also, because of an excellent relationship with their trusted tax advisor; someone who fulfilled the role of educator, advocate and steward of their resources; they were able to achieve short term and long term goals faster than the norm, by paying attention to their tax advantages.

Consistency factored prominently into their strategy. Each time as they revisited their goals, the process they used remained the same. Three financial documents provided accurate reporting and opportunity for analysis:

1. Their progress towards their long term *Wealth Purpose* was measurable against their Personal and Family Net Worth Statements, year over year.

2. They knew their *Tax Strategy*; by understanding their tax returns and achieving tax efficiency with a specific order of investing that all their investment advisors understood and were aligned with. They also focused on moving assets into the right "buckets" to facilitate family income splitting.

3. Finally, they jealously guarded their *Wealth Potential;* that is, what their holdings would be worth when they needed them in the future, after professional fees, interest costs and inflation

were taken into account. Future purchasing power was a key deliverable in their planning.

The truly wealthy are principled builders. They are outliers because they do certain things consistently and differently from the norm. Catherine and Chet were financial outliers. With the peace of mind that came with their strategy, process and plan, they were able to accumulate wealth and live their *Life's Purpose* along the way.

> *What's exciting about their story is that anyone can be a financial outlier.*

Following are noteworthy traits and habits financially successful families have, which you may wish to consider implementing for your family:

Financial outliers value education. Because they often have professional credentials, they embrace a culture of continuing professional development, challenging themselves to think and learn throughout their lifetimes. That makes them innovators, creative thinkers and people who embrace change.

Change is Good. To be successful in building wealth throughout your life, you will need to understand how changes in your life, the economy and the tax laws apply to your lifestyle, and affect your ability to accumulate, grow and preserve wealth. Wealthy people overcome financial obstacles and Black Swans with a strategy, plan and process.

Leverage The Money You Work With. Financial outliers understand that corporate dollars are taxed at lower rates than personal dollars. They are deliberate about planning the level of their income year over year, ensuring adequacy to meet their lifestyle needs, and inflation adjusting, but avoiding tax waste. They leverage the larger corporate dollars to make expenditures critical to their success at work and in life. For example, they negotiate for:

- Group insurance: to mitigate costs relating to health care and insurance
- Transportation: a new car, but reporting personal use of the vehicle
- Meals and entertainment: with a 50% allocation for personal consumption
- Memberships to social and athletic clubs

- Access to employer-provided loans at low interest rates: for investing in equity at the firm or in the financial markets, or to fund mortgage debt
- Education costs: access to a tax free benefit through an employer-funded education

Avoid Tax Waste. The truly wealthy will arrange their affairs within the framework of the law to pay average rates of taxes; not high rates of tax. In the future, it is expected that top marginal tax rates will confiscate more than 50% of income in some provinces; marginal tax rates can also be over 50% for families subject to income-tested clawbacks of social benefits and credits. Families which become financial outliers overcome high taxation by ensuring:

- Withholding taxes are correct, and not over-deducted. The compromise is a negligible tax refund in the spring. The great advantage is the opportunity to invest into the marketplace and the right "money buckets" with the extra cash all year long.
- Earnings – both active and passive – beat the rate of inflation. This requires annual inflation adjusting of wages and benefits.
- Income sources are diversified to average down the overall marginal tax rates on all income.
- Both income and assets are as evenly split with family members as possible.
- At least 18% of earnings are invested, up to allowable contribution maximums, in Registered Pension Plans and/or Registered Retirement Savings Plans; thereafter into tax preferred investment opportunities.
- Tax savings resulting from RRSPs and other tax deductions are invested into the Tax Free Savings Account (TFSA), topping up to the maximum contribution room for every family member every year, or other tax advantaged investments, including life insurance.
- Other capital assets are acquired, "on sale" if possible, to ensure real values accrue faster than the rate of inflation. They understand that accrued values in non-registered assets are not subject to tax until disposition, which is a big advantage as well.
- The expensive costs of non-deductible debt are shut down; in fact, banking options are put into place to auto pay consumer credit card balances every month. Other debt may be acquired, but not

in the absence of a definitive debt repayment plan, and with an eye to tax deductibility.

- All taxes are paid on time: income taxes, sales taxes, payroll remittances, and instalment remittances to avoid expensive interest and penalties.

Financial outliers understand that the possession of an abundance of money requires a business-like focus, rather than an emotional focus. Because of this, they can plan for some of life's most powerful financial moments with purpose and finesse. One of those moments is the moment just before death. That's when the fair market value of assets must be reported for tax purposes.

Planning to minimize taxation when assets change hands from one generation to the next must begin many years beforehand. While nothing is certain but death and taxes, the fact is, only one of the two certainties has a definitive deadline. It comes once a year. The deadline for the other is less predictable.

That's why families must be able to discuss whether assets will be transferred during a taxpayer's lifetime or at death, at adjusted cost base or fair market value, as the case may be. Multi-generational tax and investment planning keeps wealth in the family and can bring extreme wealth to the next generations. That can either be a burden or an incredible empowerment, with the right principles, process and plans.

The Money Moral

Early in this book we asked you to tell us your number: How much is enough? When you get there, and it might be sooner than you think, don't forget to give yourself permission to work on the impact you want your life to have.

Financial outliers give themselves permission to live their Life Purpose along their financial way. They are average people, who become truly wealthy, cherishing their financial freedom for a specific reason: *to live a happy, purposeful life.*

ESSENTIAL FAMILY
TAX FACTS

I hope that this book has given you an opportunity to Know More and Keep More so you can achieve your Wealth Purpose with a Tax Strategy. Following are Family Tax Facts useful in gathering family tax documents for tax season.

Sincerely,

Evelyn

The Details: Read these Essential Family Tax Facts

The Tools: Check out Knowledge Bureau's Income Tax Estimator and The Eight Minute Educator – Watch It Online at **www.knowledgebureau.com/newsbooks**

Learn Like a Pro and Help Others: Take certificate courses in tax, bookkeeping and wealth management online. See **www.knowledgebureau.com** or call for assistance: 1-866-953-4769.

Changes to Tax Brackets and Rates

The federal tax brackets have been indexed for inflation. The indexing factor for brackets and personal amounts that are indexed is calculated as the average monthly consumer price index for the twelve months ending September 30 of the previous tax year divided by the average monthly consumer price index for the twelve months ending September 30 of the second preceding tax year.

The indexation factor for 2015 is 1.7% for 2016 the factor is 1.3%.

2015 Brackets	2015 Rates	2016 Brackets	2016 Rates
Up to $11,327	0	Up to $11,474	0
$11,328 to $44,701	15%	$11,475 to $45,282	15%
$44,702 to $89,401	22%	$45,283 to $90,563	20.5%
$89,402 to $138,586	26%	$90,564 to $140,388	26%
Over $138,586	29%	$140,389 to $200,000	29%
		Over $200,000	33%

These tax brackets are important to know as they will help you understand how to optimize pension income splitting options, stay under Old Age Security clawbacks and other income testing thresholds. Note that provincial brackets will vary from the federal ones.

Marginal Tax Rates

All income sources are not taxed alike. The marginal tax rates – what you'll pay on the next dollars you earn – are usually changed annually by federal and provincial budgets. Knowing your marginal tax rate helps you plan to diversify your income sources. Be sure to stay tuned to the changes by subscribing to *Knowledge Bureau Report at www.knowledgebureau.com.*

Federal Non-Refundable Tax Credits – Personal Amounts

Rates for 2016 are estimated as official numbers had not yet been released at the time of publication.

Personal Amounts		2015	2016
Basic Personal Amount	Maximum Claim[1]	$11,327	$11,474
Age Amount	Maximum Claim[1]	$7,033	$7,124
	Reduced by net income over[1]	$35,466	$35,927
Spouse or Common-Law Partner Amount	Not infirm[1]	$11,327	$11,474
	Infirm[1]	$13,420	$13,594
Eligible Child under 18	Not infirm[1]	$0	$0
	Infirm (Family Caregiver)[1]	$2,093	$2,120
Amount for Eligible Dependants	Not infirm[1]	$11,327	$11,474
	Infirm[1]	$13,420	$13,594
Amount for Infirm Dependants	Maximum Claim[1]	$6,700	$6,787
	Reduced by net income over[1]	$6,720	$6,807
Pension Income Amount	Maximum Claim	$2,000	$2,000
Adoption Expenses	Maximum Claim[1]	$15,255	$15,453
Caregiver Amount	Not infirm[1]	$4,608	$4,668
	Infirm[1]	$6,701	$6,788
	Reduced by net income over[1]	$15,735	$15,940
Disability Amount	Basic Amount[1]	$7,899	$8,002
	Supplementary Amount[1]	$4,607	$4,667
	Base Child Care Amount[1]	$2,699	$2,734
Tuition and Education Amounts +Textbook Tax Credit	Minimum Tuition	$100	$100
	Full-time Education Amt. (per month)	$400 +$65	$400 +$65
	Part-time Education Amt. (per month)	$120 +$20	$120 +$20
Medical Expenses	3% limitation[1]	$2,208	$2,237
Refundable Medical Expense Credit	Maximum[1]	$1,172	$1,187
	Base Family Income[1]	$25,939	$26,276
	Minimum earned income[1]	$3,421	$3,465
Donation Credit	Low-rate ceiling	$200	$200
First-Time Donations	Rate	25%	25%
	Maximum Donation	$1,000	$1,000
Canada Employment Amount	Maximum[1]	$1,146	$1,161
Children's Fitness Amount[2]	Maximum	N/A	N/A
Home Buyers' Amount	Maximum	$5,000	$5,000
Children's Arts Amount	Maximum	$500	$500
Volunteer Firefighters		$3,000	$3,000
Volunteer Search and Rescue		$3,000	$3,000
Home Accessibility Tax Credit	Maximum claim	$10,000	$10,000

[1] These amounts are indexed
[2] Children's Fitness Amount converted to a refundable credit for 2015 and subsequent years

INDEX